T0203473

MANGO

Edile

Series Editor: Andrew F. Smith

EDIBLE is a revolutionary series of books dedicated to food and drink
that explores the rich history of cuisine. Each book reveals the global
history and culture of one type of food or beverage.

Already published

Mango

A Global History

*Constance L. Kirker and
Mary Newman*

REAKTION BOOKS

For mangovores the world over

Published by Reaktion Books Ltd
Unit 32, Waterside
44–48 Wharf Road
London N1 7UX, UK
www.reaktionbooks.co.uk

First published 2024
Copyright © Constance L. Kirker and Mary Newman 2024

All rights reserved

No part of this publication may be reproduced, stored in a retrieval
system, or transmitted, in any form or by any means, electronic,
mechanical, photocopying, recording or otherwise, without the prior
permission of the publishers

Printed and bound in India by Replika Press Pvt. Ltd

A catalogue record for this book is available from the British Library

ISBN 978 1 78914 915 9

Contents

Introduction

There is a good chance that if you live in the United States or Europe, you have never seen a tree full of ripe mangoes. It is possible that you don't even have a mango recipe in your recipe collection. Many of us are now learning of the pleasures of the bright, intense flavour of mangoes in smoothies and cocktails, but we are also noticing the relatively sad and antiseptic form in which mangoes are presented in supermarkets, neatly cut and packaged tightly in clear-plastic containers or bags. But, as every mango-lover will tell you, the total experience of smell, touch, taste and texture is the very point of a mango. The consumption of a ripe, fresh mango is a 'full body experience'. Mangoes inspire passion. Mango-lovers in all countries where the fruit thrives have learned how to prolong the enjoyment of mangoes by pickling, drying and preserving them.

Though many mango products are now available worldwide, especially in today's connected world, ecstatic praise for fresh mangoes makes people in the Western world a bit uncomfortable. Americans, for example, are used to assuming they have access to all the best things on the planet, including the finest, most sought-after foods, but most mangoes imported to the United States are pale imitations of the real thing. The American mango is often a bland disappointment. Most Europeans are more likely to have encountered one of the 16,000 Mango

Mango vendor in Kerala, India.

retail clothing stores than to have eaten an imported Indian Alphonso mango. What are we missing?

To get the fullest enjoyment out of eating a mango, we must step out of our comfort zones and get messy. But Western culture has a definite bias against mess or disorder. Eating with our hands, actually touching our food, is not customary, while in many parts of the world where mangoes grow, this is traditional and acceptable. It may be that the bias goes back to Aristotle and his theory of the hierarchy of the senses, in which sight and sound are privileged, while smell, touch and taste are relegated to the realm of the lower senses. Of course, it might be noted that the Greeks and the Romans actually ate with their hands. Forks are a European invention and were not widely used until the 1500s. The aversion to touching our food resulted in countless types of eating utensils, including a Victorian-era mango fork.

This book explores the properties of mangoes through the lens of the five senses. You can't judge a book by its cover, or a mango by its colour. The skin colour is no indication of ripeness or taste. Mangoes are not uniform in size, colour, taste, smell or texture, so the rules that are used in the West to select and

Sofía Sánchez
Barrenechea
wearing the
Mango dress
at the Met
Gala, 2019.

prepare other fruits do not apply. Clearly, there is a lot to learn about mangoes!

Mango-lovers who find themselves far away from where their desired variety grows during mango season will go to great trouble and expense to locate one, even planning a family trip thousands of miles away from home to obtain their coveted mango. A popular website was developed to cater to the nostalgia of Indian customers who have moved away from their family homes and places of origin and who yearn for the perfect mango of their memories.[1] On the site, author Salman Rushdie could order the Fern mango pickles from his childhood that inspired the pickle factory in his 1981 prize-winning novel *Midnight's Children*. Pakistani-American communities

Range of colours of mango, Brixton Market, London.

can use WhatsApp to contact Farm Fresh founder Zulfikar Momin, who sources desired mango varieties from South Asia and delivers them directly to airports in the United States.[2]

The early cultural history of mango is not to be found in sources most familiar to Westerners, such as Greek and Roman mythology, Judaeo-Christian references, Shakespeare or the Western literary canon. But the fruit does have deep connections to the beliefs and practices of religions of South Asia – Hinduism, Buddhism and Jainism – both in the past and the present. There are references to mangoes in written documents that were first oral traditions, such as the *Puranas* and *Vedas*, and the Hindu epic tales, the *Ramayana* and the *Mahabharata*.

One of the fascinating aspects of this mango passion in countries where the fruit thrives is the vibrant literary tradition the fruit has spawned, both historical and contemporary. Mango-lovers write about mangoes expressively and vividly. Mangoes appear in stories from ancient folk tales to contemporary children's books in which the fruit serves as a metaphor to teach life lessons. Mangoes function as an effective 'gateway' food for children, introducing them to stories from a variety of cultures, from India and the Philippines to African nations. Famous South Asian poets, such as Urdu poet Mirza Ghalib, extolled mangoes; explorers, such as the fourteenth-century traveller Ibn Battuta, noted mangoes in their journals; contemporary culinary memoirs detail mango family traditions.

Mango is the only fruit that has its own literary genre, known somewhat derisively as 'sari-mango' literature. Writers of the Indian diaspora, as well as those who have left homes in Africa, the Caribbean, Mexico and the Philippines, use mango imagery when referencing their nostalgia for the pleasures of their homelands that they most miss. References to mangoes immediately bring to mind the 'exotic'. Mangoes are sexy. All fruits are sexy, but mango is the only fruit that has a position in the *Kama Sutra* named for it. Gauguin's paintings of Tahitian women and mangoes are unmistakably sensual.

Horticultural writings of the Mughals, Portuguese explorers and Jesuit missionaries detail the varieties of mangoes and grafting techniques and how the cultivation of this fruit spread throughout the world. The Portuguese encountered mangoes in their explorations of South Asia in the 1500s. They proceeded to introduce this delicious fruit through trade routes around East Africa, West Africa and, along with the slave trade, eventually crossing the Atlantic Ocean to the Caribbean and South America. Tropical fruits were introduced into their colonies in the Caribbean islands by the British, French and Spanish, who were searching for possible sites where these valuable food sources might flourish. Exotic foodstuffs like mango began to arrive by ship from the Caribbean to ports in the United States during the American colonial period beginning in the 1750s. To preserve these delicate fruits, they were immediately made into pickles, chutneys and jams.

The Indian Mughal emperors who ruled between the 1500s and 1700s were avid mango fans. There are detailed accounts of their gardens, orchards and culinary traditions. Recipes featuring mangoes were developed by royal chefs and are still on offer today in fine dining and speciality restaurants. The Mughal emperors named favourite varieties, and Mughal royal patronage of horticulture led to thousands of grafted varieties. The politics of gifting mangoes, which was documented during the time of these rulers, is alive and well today. Even during the COVID-19 pandemic of 2020–21, India sent crates of top-quality mangoes to embassies abroad.

According to her former chef John Higgins, Britain's Queen Elizabeth II so enjoyed mangoes that on any day, 'she could tell you how many mangoes were in the fridge at Buckingham Palace.'[3] Queen Elizabeth II was not the first British monarch

Paul Gauguin, *Woman with Mango*, 1892, oil on canvas.

to be enthralled with mangoes. A memorable scene in the film *Victoria and Abdul* shows Abdul presenting mangoes that had been sent as a gift from India to Queen Victoria. Unfortunately, the mangoes had gone bad. It wasn't until 1931 that London received its first shipment of fresh mangoes. During the period of the British Raj, when India represented the jewel in the crown of the empire, the wives of British government civil servants, *memsahibs*, referred to this local fruit as the 'bathroom fruit' because it was so messy to consume. They did develop a taste for preserved mangoes as chutneys. Intrepid Victorian lady travellers Lady Brassey and Lady Callcott mention in their travel journals occasions on which they were treated to mangoes. Marianne North (1830–1890) documented her travels, painting the mangoes she enjoyed in Brazil and India. She included these illustrations among the more than nine hundred paintings she gifted to the Royal Botanic Gardens, Kew in London.

Mangoes played a part in Mao's Cultural Revolution in China. In 1968 Pakistan's foreign minister gifted a box of mangoes to Chairman Mao, who then passed them on as a reward to workers and students for their revolutionary valour. The preserved magical fruit, yet unknown in northern China at the time, became a treasured icon. Just as surprising is the story of space mangoes. In 2017 mango seeds were sent on a 33-day trip aboard a Chinese spacecraft. Chinese scientists claim they have recently made progress in the country's space plant-breeding programme, searching for genetically superior mango varieties propagated from these mango seeds. One of the most expensive mangoes in the world, Miyazaki, or Egg of the Sun, is cultivated in Japan. Prize examples are auctioned for thousands of U.S. dollars annually and are considered a fine delicacy.

There are both challenges and opportunities that will shape the future of mangoes. Growers, governments, private

Amanda Almira Newton, *Bennett Alphonso Mango*, 1908, watercolour illustration for the USDA Pomological Watercolor Collection.

organizations and researchers are working on introducing mango products to new consumers as well as exploring new varieties of mango. Finding uses for all the waste involved in mango processing and consumption is also an area of interest. The major thrust of many initiatives is improving the local mango producers' livelihoods by providing education and resources.

Readers will learn how and why mangoes are a universally adored, even iconic, food in the places where they grow. It can be argued that no one fruit in the culinary experience of the Western world sparks a similar shared passion, emotional connection or response.

While the most renowned varieties of fresh mango may not be available most of the year or in every supermarket, preserved mango, dried, tinned and pickled can be found virtually everywhere. We hope on these pages you will learn something new about the mangoes you already love or be nudged to experiment with a new food experience – even if it's very messy and outside your comfort zone.

I

Magnificent Mango: Botany, Production and Health

Comparisons of fossilized mango leaves dating from 60 million years ago with modern-day mango species have led palaeo-ethnobotanists to conclude that the origin of mango lies in northeast India. From there, the fruit spread to South India and Southeast Asia.[1] Analysis of grinding stones and pottery dating from 1500 BCE and belonging to the Harappans, the oldest civilization on the Indian subcontinent dating to 1500 BCE, revealed traces of mango. Mango fibres were even found on human teeth at Harappan archaeological sites.[2]

As mangoes spread to southern India, the word *amra-phal*, referring to the mango, became *aam-kaay* in the Tamil language. Pronunciation differences resulted in the word *maamkaay*, which the Malayali people in the area of India now known as Kerala further evolved to *maanga*. When the Portuguese settled in Kerala in the sixteenth century and encountered the fruit, they called it 'mango'.

The botanical name for mango is *Mangifera indica*, meaning 'an Indian plant bearing mangoes'. There are about 49 other species in the genus *Mangifera* but most of them do not produce edible-quality fruit and are usually referred to as 'wild

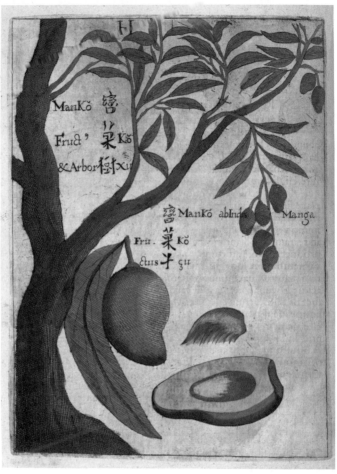

Mango illustration from Michał Boym, *Flora sinensis* (1656).

mangoes'. The original wild mangoes were very small, with little edible flesh. Scientists have an interest in wild mangoes as they may provide genetic material to aid in improving the isease and pest resistance of today's commercial varieties of mangoes.[3]

Mangoes are a stone fruit classified as a drupe. Drupes have edible flesh surrounding a fibrous, hard stone that contains a single seed. The mango seed may be either mono-embryonic (classified as Indian) or poly-embryonic (classified as Indo-Chinese). Fruits from mono-embryonic seeds must be propagated by grafting because a tree grown from the seed will vary from the parent tree. A poly-embryonic seed has many embryos that are similar to the parent tree, and thus can be grown from seed and be true to the parent plant.[4]

The genus *Mangifera* is a member of the Anacardiaceae family, which includes cashews, poison ivy, poison oak, sumac and pistachio. The plants in this family contain the oily compound urushiol, which causes an allergic reaction in some people.[5] The most common reaction is a form of contact dermatitis called 'mango rash'.

While it is possible to grow a mango tree in a pot from the kernel, it will take years for it to fruit, and it may never produce fruit unless all the growing conditions, including temperature, water and humidity, are suitable. Mangoes are grown in tropical and subtropical locations in more than one hundred countries, with varying success. Because of their climate requirements, mangoes can only grow in limited areas of the United States: in

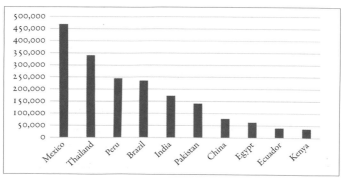

Top mango-exporting countries (in tonnes).

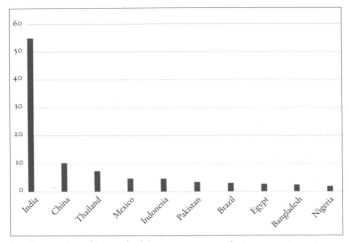

Production share (per cent) of the top mango-producing countries, using data taken from the National Mango Database 2020.

Florida, California and Hawaii and in the U.S. territory of Puerto Rico. In Europe, mangoes can grow in several micro-climates, such as in Sicily and Málaga.

India produces about half of the world's mangoes, over 24 million tonnes in 2020, according to data from the Food and Agriculture Organization of the United Nations.[6] However, only 173,000 tonnes are exported (30 per cent of which goes to the United Arab Emirates and Saudi Arabia); the rest are used for domestic consumption. Pakistan produces only one-tenth of the amount that India does, but it exports four times more, with most going to the European Union (EU). Brazil and Peru also supply the EU market. Mexico is one of the world's largest exporters, at 468,000 tonnes, with 90 per cent of its exports going to the United States. Guatemala, Nicaragua, Brazil, Peru and Costa Rica also supplement the U.S. market with complementary growing seasons to provide nearly year-round availability. After the EU and the USA, China is the third leading importer of mangoes, mostly from Vietnam and Thailand.

Trade agreements between various countries specify that before fresh mangoes may be exported and imported, they must be processed by dipping them into hot water or using other phytosanitation measures such as radiation or chemical treatment to ensure they are free of pests, bacteria and diseases. Developing countries often do not have the facilities to process mangoes for exportation. In addition, some varieties do not hold up well during transportation and are thus not part of the export market. Mangoes that are not exported as fresh fruit are often processed in their home countries by drying or pickling, or turned into purée or juice, and then exported.

Mango trees begin to produce fruit two to four years after planting. Fruits dangle from branches on long, slender stems. Crucial to a successful mango harvest in India are pre-monsoon rains from March through April, known as 'mango showers' or 'mango rain'. They help in the ripening of mangoes and prevent the fruit from prematurely dropping off the trees. The

Dried chilli mango, a favourite flavour pairing.

appearance of mango blossoms heralds the arrival of spring, and mango trees laden with fruit are the essence of summer.

Mangoes can be eaten in their green immature state as well as their mature state. Unripe, immature mangoes will taste sour. They are often preserved by pickling in salt or vinegar with oil and spices added, depending on regional tastes and availability. Amchur is mango powder that is made from unripe, young mangoes and is a common ingredient in Indian cooking. This powder can also be used in a marinade.

Mature mangoes are consumed in various ways around the world in both sweet and savoury dishes. In some regions, fully

Mango tree canopy, Hawaii.

ripe mangoes are pickled. A favourite Thai dessert is mango with sticky rice. In savoury dishes, mango is often paired with chilli peppers.

Mango fruit purées and flavourings have applications in the processing of a variety of food items including wines, teas, ice creams, breakfast cereals, baby food, confectionery and biscuits. The peel, or skin, of the mango is edible and packed with nutrients including vitamins, fibre and antioxidants. Mango peel powder added to baked goods increases the fibre content and makes use of a part of the mango that is normally considered waste. The peel and pit can be boiled with sugar to make a syrup that can be used in cocktails. Though it may offer health benefits, mango peel contains compounds that may also cause allergic reactions in some individuals. The peel has an unpleasant bitter taste, and it may contain traces of pesticide residues.

The fragrance of the fruit is a more important factor in selecting a ripe mango than the colour of the peel. Advances in technology suggest that 'e-noses' (electronic instruments) could become widely used to determine ripeness, removing the more subjective human element.

The mango tree is more than a source of fruit. The dense, cool, shady area underneath the lush canopy of a mango tree often serves as a space for meetings, resting and even romantic trysts. 'Under the Mango Tree' is the title of several books and poems. Trees typically grow anywhere from 10 to 30 metres (30 to 100 ft) high, and are often characterized by a broad, rounded canopy that may extend 30–38 metres (100–125 ft) in width. There are also some other varieties that are more upright with an oval, less extensive canopy. Horticulturalists have developed dwarf varieties such as the Rapoza, which are known in retail nurseries as 'condo mangos' for home gardens.

Mango trees are long-lived and relatively fast-growing – under ideal conditions a tree can grow up to 2 m (6 ft 6 in.) in its first year. The oldest known mango tree in Asia grows in the city of Thakurgaon in Bangladesh and is believed to be between 150 and 300 years old.

While there are several insect pests and diseases that may affect mango trees in commercial orchards, most of them can be managed with pesticide applications. Some common pests are scale insects, tip borers, fruit flies, seed weevils, seed caterpillars, termites and fruit-piercing moths. Growing mangoes organically is preferred for the baby food market in particular.

When mango trees no longer fruit, their wood and bark are still useful products. The wood may be made into furniture or musical instruments such as ukuleles; spalted mango wood is particularly attractive for this purpose, with interesting designs created by a fungus that grows on the wood. The burgeoning mango wood furniture industry provides farmers with incentives to cut down non-productive trees and plant new seedlings. The wood is also used as fuel for barbecue, although this usage is controversial because mangoes are in the same family as poison ivy, and urushiol can be spread by the smoke.

There are some differences in leaf size and shape among mango varieties but generally leaves have a long, oval shape. They are glossy dark green on the surface with a lighter green underside. The seasonal new growth of leaves is known as 'flushing' and appears in a distinct pinkish-purple colour. Young leaves are edible after being boiled to soften them and are served as a vegetable. Mango leaf powder may be added to foods or drinks as a source of vitamins and antioxidants. Dried mango leaves are enjoyed as a tea or infusion.

Other parts of the mango tree are also edible. The flowers produce nectar that bees collect and turn into mango honey. The seed may be boiled or baked and is eaten as a vegetable in some parts of India. Seeds can also be incorporated into recipes to add flavour to a dish or used to create mango-infused

Leaf new growth, or flushing.   Mango flowers.

alcohol for cocktails. In a recipe created by the Culinary Institute of America, a traditional Mexican mole sauce is flavoured by simmering the sauce with mango seeds.

Varieties

Mangoes vary widely depending on size, shape, colour, taste, smell and feel (that is, the texture or tactility of fibres or lack of fibres). The best way to consume some varieties is by sucking the flesh out of the mango, thus completing the entire sensory experience with the addition of this distinctive sound.

The average weight of different mango fruit varieties ranges from less than 80 grams (3 oz) to more than 800 grams (1 lb 12 oz). Fruit size varies from 5 centimetres (2 in.) to 25 centimetres (10 in.). It has been reported that on the small Caribbean island of Nevis, mangoes can grow as large as a human head. Fruit can weigh from 100 grams (4 oz) to 2 kilograms (4 lb), but the *Guinness World Records 2022* cites a mango from Colombia weighing 4.25 kilograms (9 lb), the size and weight

Poster for Fairchild Garden's mango festival, Miami.

of a bowling ball. One of the largest common varieties is the Palmer, weighing just under a kilogram (2 lb).

Many mangoes are teardrop-shaped but some varieties are oval, round or somewhat lopsided in form. The Guatemalan mango de leche is round, while the Haitian Francisque is flat. The Totapuri has a distinctive oblong shape with pointy ends. The Kilichundan variety literally means 'beak of a bird', a nod to its distinctive shape. The Philippine Carabao mango is somewhat heart-shaped and, as the official national fruit, is said to symbolize the kindness in the heart of every Filipino.

Both the flesh and the peel of mangoes appear in a stunning range of colours. The fruit flesh can vary from pale yellow to deepest orange. The Kesar variety is named for its flesh colour, as *kesar* means 'saffron' in Hindi. In the 2012 documentary film *The Fruit Hunters*, horticulturists Noris Ledesma and Richard Campbell travelled to Indonesia to collect mango samples for the Fairchild Botanical Garden in Coral Gables, Florida. The mango specialists were searching for a rare mango with white flesh found in Bali known as 'Wani' or 'White Mango'. This mango is known as *binjai* in Brunei, where it is used to make a dipping sauce for *ambuyat*, the country's national dish, derived from the interior trunk of the sago palm.

The skin of the mango can appear in an even wider range of colours, from greens through yellows, reds and blues, often with multiple colours on a single mango. A rare mango from Indonesia called Kastoree (Kastooree or Kasturi), nicknamed the 'blue mango', has a purple-blue, waxy skin that contrasts vividly with its deep pumpkin-orange flesh. Much to the disdain of mango-lovers in countries where the fruit thrives and has long been cherished, the American market has favoured only the reddish variety. But Americans are slowly being introduced to the mango rainbow. Mango selection for the consumer is complicated because the skin colour does not necessarily indicate ripeness; confusion arises especially for Westerners, who often buy fruit based on colour.

While sweetness can be a subjective element of taste, the Brix number is an objective measurement of sweetness. A Brix reading measures total sugar concentration of the fruit; the higher the Brix number, the sweeter the fruit. The sweetness increases as a mango ripens. The Carabao mango from the Philippines has been listed in the *Guinness World Records* since 1995 as the sweetest mango.

In addition to sweetness, a mango can have underlying hints of sourness and pine, and a range of tastes from floral to citrusy depending on the variety, or its terroir. The term 'terroir' refers either to the unique set of characteristics of environment in which a food product is produced or those characteristics associated properly with a food product, which it derives from the soil of its particular location. It is often suggested that a mango tastes like a cross between a peach and other fruits, notably pineapple, orange, lemon or lime. Coconut Cream is an appropriately named variety developed and grown in

Kasturi mango variety.

Device for measuring sweetness on the Brix scale.

Florida, as is the Ice Cream variety in Trinidad, which tastes like a mango sorbet.

Some mango varieties are named after the locations in which they are grown, such as the Manila Mango. They can also be named after people, such as the Florida variety Irwin, named after botanist F. D. Irwin, who developed the variety in 1939. Zill is named for another Florida botanist, Lawrence Zill. Other varieties are also named to honour individuals: the Haden variety, one of the most widely cultivated in the world, was

Kaleem Ullah Khan, known as the 'Mango Man', shows how he grafts
different varieties of mangoes at his farm in Malihabad, India.

developed in Florida and named by Florence Haden to honour
her husband, Captain John Haden.

A long history of grafting efforts by botanists worldwide
has resulted in thousands of mango varieties. When Portuguese
Jesuit missionaries came to India in 1542 and established a colony in Goa, they fell in love with the mango. Although mangoes
had been in cultivation long before their arrival, the Jesuits
helped boost production and created new varieties through
scientific grafting. The Mughal emperor Akbar, interested in
Western/European learning, including agricultural techniques,
was impressed with the Jesuits' knowledge of grafting, wel-
comed them to his court and encouraged their efforts. Later
Mughal emperors introduced many new varieties, and Goa
soon became a leading exporter of mangoes to the rest of India
and the world. Some of the varieties developed by the Jesuits
have meaningful names: 'Xavier' named in honour of St Francis
Xavier, co-founder of the Jesuits, and 'Hilario', named for a
sixteenth-century Jesuit grafter, Hilario Fernandes.

One of the most famous mango experts today is Kaleem Ullah Khan from Malihabad, Uttar Pradesh, India. Known worldwide as the 'Mango Man', 82-year-old Khan lives on a mango tree orchard started by his father. A conservator of these heritage trees, he has a special, reverential relationship with a particular mango tree that is at least 120 years old. He started grafting new varieties onto the tree in the 1980s, and by 2022 had created more than three hundred varieties on this single tree, with a wide range of tastes, colours, sizes and aromas.[7]

In many Western cultures, the taste of mature mangoes is considered 'exotic' or 'tropical', while unripe mangoes have been described as tasting citrusy and tart. Food writers and chefs Doreen Gamboa Fernandez and Gilda Fernando explain how Filipino cuisine features this mango sourness in *sinigang*, a sour savoury soup.[8] Pickled mangoes can range in taste from sweet to sour. The Thai sweet green mango tastes similar to a crisp Granny Smith apple, but with unique non-tropical flavours, nutty with slightly floral notes.

Much has been written about the quest to find the best-tasting mango variety. Many Indians prefer the Alphonso variety, while others think the Alphonso has merely benefitted from effective marketing. Kesar mango has its champions and is one of the most expensive and popular varieties in India. Varying widely in taste and texture, different mango varieties are suited for different culinary uses. Personal preferences for a particular sweet, juicy and ripe mango variety can depend on nostalgia for the fruit of childhood memories. India researcher David Shulman, in his article 'The Scent of Memory in Hindu South India', makes the case, using the aroma of mango, that 'to smell is to remember' and 'in India, one smells his way back into his past.'[9]

Researchers have detected over 270 volatile chemical compounds in mangoes, including esters, which give it a fruity aroma, and specific compounds very similar to those that create the aromas of strawberries and coconut.[10] Certain mango varieties are named for their scent, such as the Puerto Rican variety Turpentine. Several chemicals in the terpene category have been found in mangoes, giving them a distinctive turpentine aroma.[11] The 'funky' smell of the pungent *Mangifera odorata* is considered by some to be an attractive quality. A mango variety found in Thailand, Nam Dok Mai, is particularly fragrant.

Texture plays an important role in the enjoyment of mangoes, from the stringy fibrous varieties to those described as creamy, with champions of each vigorously advocating for their preferences. Several varieties, such as Edward, Mallika, Keitt and Irwin, have been developed specifically to have minimal fibres. Traditionalists, however, see the fibres as a vital part of the visceral experience of mango-eating.

The juicy quality of a mango is an important element. Poet Urvi Kumbhat tells us, 'There is no mango without its mess.' Joanna Chen, chef and writer, notes, 'What I crave is the tactility.'[12] Often when mangoes are mentioned in the literature of the Indian diaspora, for example, writers note with nostalgia the drippy, sticky eating experience and bemoan the dry, crunchy, apple-like texture of American packaged mangoes.

Some varieties of mango, such as Alphonso, Dussehri and Kesar, have earned worldwide recognition because of their unique characteristics of taste, aroma and flavour, stemming from the terroir of the locations in which these mangoes are grown. The World Trade Organization has given some varieties a Geographical Indication (GI tag) status to designate that they are only grown in specific geographic locations. The tag is viewed as an indicator of high quality and is an important marketing tool. There are ten mango varieties with the GI status in India, with several others in the process of acquiring the designation.

Health Benefits of Mangoes

Mangoes have long been a staple in the practice of Ayurvedic medicine and in the pharmacopeia of Indigenous cultures. According to Ayurvedic medicine, the human body consists of seven elements: blood, bone, fat, plasma, marrow, flesh and sexual essence. Mangoes can nourish *shudra dhatu*, sexual essence, enhancing male virility and human reproductive health. There is science to back up the anecdotes, since mangoes do contain compounds that mimic oestrogen and help to regulate sex hormones. For more than 4,000 years the various components of mangoes have been utilized to treat hypertension, insomnia, rheumatism, liver disorders, asthma and a host of other ailments, even including treating rabid dog bites.

While evidence of the health claims for mango has often been anecdotal, some studies suggest these claims may be valid. For example, a study of mango stem bark extract (MSBE), developed in Cuba under the brand name Vimang, demonstrated that MSBE had an antioxidant effect beneficial to patients suffering from cancer, diabetes and several other medical conditions.[13]

Mangoes are often listed as a superfood in popular culture; indeed, modern medicine has recognized that there are many health benefits to be derived from mangoes.[14] In a 2019 study cited in *Medicina*, researchers found that extracts of mango leaf could be useful in managing diabetes by reducing fats and glucose levels in the blood.[15]

Mangoes are also rich in vitamins and minerals. A cup of sliced mango contains 60.1 mg of vitamin C, a hefty dose considering the U.S. Food and Drug Administration daily recommendation for men is 90 mg and for women is 75 mg. Mangoes contain beta carotene, which converts to vitamin A in the body; vitamin A is known to boost the body's immune system.[16]

Health providers know that increasing potassium and decreasing sodium in the body can help to reduce hypertension. Mangoes are a good source of potassium. Also, the combination of fibre, potassium and vitamins found in mangoes is therapeutic for the arteries, thereby potentially reducing the risk of heart disease. Mangoes add copper, calcium and iron to a healthy diet, as well as antioxidants such as zeaxanthin, which may act to prevent damage to the eye from macular degeneration, a serious condition that worsens with age.

Mangoes appeal to each of our five senses: taste, sight, sound, smell and touch. Mangoes can bring about intense nostalgia for a missing childhood treat or even feelings of national or regional pride. The mango is the designated national fruit of eleven countries. Eating a mango can trigger the sensation of happiness and joy, according to neuroscientists who research how we make choices about the foods we eat.

Mangoes are a magnificent, universally adored, even iconic food in the tropical and subtropical world where they grow. It can be argued that there is no single fruit in the culinary experience of the Western world, Europe or America that sparks a shared passion, emotional connection or response like that of the mango in countries where it has a long cultural history.

2

Mango Movement

Though the mango tree is grown in more than a hundred countries across the world today, it does not move easily on its own. The large seed of this drupe, a stone fruit, cannot be carried by the wind or by birds. The tree requires a tropical climate to produce fruit, and transporting the seedlings by ship requires live specimens. Mango was one of the more difficult plants to transport during the Age of Exploration from the fifteenth to the seventeenth century at the time of the Columbian Exchange, when plants were purposely moved between the Old and the New World; once the seeds dried out, they could not germinate, and the salty ocean water was harmful to them. The Portuguese carried mangoes as ripe fruit, seedlings and later as grafted plants from West Africa to Brazil and beyond. With the 1829 invention of the Wardian case, an airtight wooden box that allowed transpiration inside to provide sufficient moisture to keep plants alive, movement of mangoes to Western countries became more reliable.[1]

Sources often say the Portuguese discovered the mango in the course of their explorations along the coast of India in the fifteenth century, a statement which might be criticized today as 'Columbusizing', that is, 'discovering' something that is not new. Many sources also report that one of the most prized varieties of mango, the Alphonso, was named after Afonso de

Wardian case for enabling the safe transit of plants on long sea voyages.

Albuquerque (*c.* 1453–1515), a Portuguese general who helped establish Portuguese colonies in India, including Goa, where excellent-quality mangoes are cultivated today. There are two other theories for the source of the name of this fibrous but tasty variety, which was the result of the grafting efforts of the Portuguese Jesuits beginning in 1575. The Jesuits were working to convert the local population to Christianity by teaching grafting techniques. It is possible that the beloved Alphonso mango was named after the horticulturist Nicolau Afonso, who grafted it around 1550, or even after the Jesuit St Alphonsus Rodriguez of Spain (1532–1617).[2] Along with the French, Spanish and English, the Portuguese rightly earned credit for the movement of mangoes through trade routes and empire building around East Africa and West Africa and eventually across the Atlantic to the Caribbean and South America.

Jesuits at Akbar's court, miniature painting by Nar Singh from the *History of Akbar* (*Akbarnama*), c. 1605.

Mangoes, Slavery and Africa

Far more significant than the movement of mango trees during the period of colonial expansion was the capture and transport of between 12 and 13 million enslaved people from Africa to the New World from 1501 to 1866. An estimated 45 per cent of them came from the central part of West Africa. One of the major trading ports in this 'triangular slave trade' (three-way transatlantic exchanges from Africa to the Americas and Europe, moving slaves, sugar and rum) on the West coast of Africa was Loango Bay, in what is today the Republic of the Congo. No structures remain to mark the tragedy of the location as a departure point for hundreds of thousands of enslaved people sent to the Americas. What does remain is a path lined by mango trees about 30 metres (100 ft) high, which is said to indicate the route the enslaved individuals took to the site of the port. There are several explanations for the existence of the trees. Possibly the mango trees grew from the dropped seeds of Africans' last meals as they were herded to the ships at the port. Another possibility is that Africans remaining on the coast planted the mango seeds in memory of those who were taken from them. It is a common practice today in some parts of Africa to plant a tree near the burial site of a loved one.[3] The shade of mango trees provides an important social focus in many African villages. Part of the UNESCO 'Routes of Enslaved Peoples: Resistance, Liberty and Heritage' Project, initiated in 1994, the path lined with mango trees was included in a tentative list of World Heritage sites in 2008.

Several sources describe a ritual involving the mango trees. 'The chained slaves made seven turns of the tree of oblivion for women or girls, nine turns for men, and the tree of return which symbolized a possible return of the spirit of the deceased to the country (Loango) once dead.'[4] This ritual of oblivion was

Row of mango trees, Kigoma Region, Tanzania.

believed to allow the slaves to forget their names and former lives in Africa.

The most important purpose of any memorial or monument is to tell a story in such a way, visually or verbally, that a particular person, thing or event will not easily be forgotten. A mango tree and memorial stone with a descriptive plaque mark the location in Africa where one of the most famous greetings in history took place. Henry Morton Stanley's question, 'Dr Livingstone, I presume?', was uttered beneath a mango tree in Ujiji on the shores of Lake Tanganyika on 10 November 1871. David Livingstone (b. 1813) died in Ujiji at age sixty in 1873, and that same huge shady mango tree existed on the very spot until 1920. Ujiji is the beginning of a long slave-trading route, stretching eastwards from the lake to Bagamoyo on the Indian

Ocean coast. By the tenth century, Arab traders had introduced mangoes to East African trade centres such as Zanzibar and Mombasa. In the sixteenth century, the Portuguese spread mangoes along the coast as an offshoot of their slave trade.

When the massive shady tree in Ujiji died, it was replaced by two mango trees grown from grafts from the original. David Livingstone was not yet thirty years old when he arrived in Africa with the goals of both saving souls and working towards sustainable development for the people of Africa. Livingstone eventually explored 47,000 kilometres (29,000 mi.) of East and Central Africa, including his search for the source of the Nile River. 'Christ, commerce and civilization' was his motto, and he was adamantly against slavery.

At one point, Livingstone was abandoned by his crew, became ill and ran out of food supplies. He was forced to rely on local edibles, including mangoes. It was not until 2014 that the details of this period came to light, including the witnessing of a horrific massacre of Africans by Arab slave traders. During these difficult times, Livingstone had been determined to continue to keep his personal field diary, intending to publish his notes in the future. With no writing paper or ink left, Livingstone recorded his daily activities on old newspapers using homemade red ink made of berry juice, which soon faded and became illegible. Livingstone died in 1873 and his diaries were eventually archived in the David Livingstone Centre in Glasgow, Scotland. In 2000, Adrian Wisnicki, a young professor in the Department of English at the University of Nebraska, used spectral imaging to bring the diaries to light. The 'Livingstone Spectral Imaging Project' was a process that involved photographing the pages under varying wavelengths of light, which then made it possible to see what the human eye could not.[5] The journals have been transcribed, digitized and made available to scholars online. We now know that Livingstone made numerous notations that spoke of mango trees as a food source in his environment.

Today mangoes are grown in East Africa and exported from Kenya and Tanzania to lucrative and growing Middle Eastern and European markets. The West African Regional Mango Alliance was formed by growers in Burkina Faso, the Ivory Coast, Gambia, Ghana, Guinea and Mali to assist production and distribution to markets. Unfortunately, much of the mango crop is wasted post-harvest because the crop ripens at the same time and farmers lack storage, transport options or an export strategy. YieldWise is an international organization within the Rockefeller Foundation, partnering with the University of Nairobi, to reduce waste throughout the food value chain. The goal is to link mango farmers and buyers supporting aggregation centres for the smaller producers, where mangoes can be graded and sent to appropriate markets.[6]

Mangoes in the New World

What happened to those enslaved Africans once they reached the New World? Delivered to the islands of the Caribbean – known as the West Indies by the colonizing European powers – the captives were compelled to serve as forced labour, working in harsh conditions on sugar plantations for a new wealthy class of white merchants and planters who profited greatly from the production and distribution of sugarcane. The work was backbreaking and the institution of slavery dehumanizing. This large labour force had to be housed and fed. The colonial powers experimented with different foods and distribution methods, including unsuccessful attempts to cultivate mangoes as a commercial food product in botanical gardens that were established on the islands. In 1758 the Society for the Encouragement of

Arts, Manufactures and Commerce (later known as the Royal Society for Arts) offered a cash prize for the first person who was able to successfully import mango seeds to England for the purpose of onward shipment to introduce cultivation of the fruit to the sugar-producing Caribbean colonies.[7]

Plantation owners came to the conclusion that allowing their slaves to cultivate their own food sources in individual provisions gardens was efficient. While mangoes never became a viable or lucrative plantation crop, enslaved people planted their individual gardens to include mango trees, coconut trees and banana plants along with vegetables to ensure sustenance for their families. As a legacy of the slavery formerly enacted in the region, hundreds of varieties of mango have evolved, and today mangoes remain widely distributed throughout the Caribbean islands.

African languages, music and dance played a vital role in the creation of the cultures of the Caribbean today. Enslaved persons from Africa secretly brought religious traditions from their homelands, including the belief in multiple deities called *orishas*. In Cuba, the West African Yoruba tradition evolved into *santería*, a syncretic religion combining *orishas* with Roman Catholic saints who were worshipped with specific food offerings. Gifts of mangoes are made to Oshun, who represents river waters and rules over marriages and fertility. Mango leaves were used in traditional healing practices. *Obeah*, the belief in black magic or sorcery, is illegal in fourteen countries or territories in the Anglophone Caribbean region.[8] Even today, bottles containing special potions meant to deter potential thieves from picking the fruit as it ripens still occasionally appear dangling from mango trees.[9]

The Spanish began planting sugarcane on the island of Cuba in 1523, but the country became the most significant producer of sugar only after the Haitian Revolution of 1791 to 1804 ended the use of slave labour in Haiti. The sugar-producing West Indian islands, including Cuba, developed into mono-crop economies, with only small provision farms providing food for the population. The Cuban people were removed from their small farms by the Spanish government's Reconcentration policy in response to their own attempts at revolution during the Spanish–American War in 1898. Cuban insurgents were forced to forage for food. An insurgent general noted that his troops survived for days by eating only mangoes.[10]

Almost one hundred years later, in 1991, during the communist rule of Fidel Castro (1926–2016) and after the dissolution of the Soviet Union, which ended the importation of food, the Cuban people endured the Special Period euphemistically called the Time of Peace, a period of economic crisis and depression between 1991 and 2000. Food shortages required the people to again live off the land. Planting mango trees in every apartment block was among the efforts to stave off starvation caused by Cuban government injunctions against private

A mango vendor waits for customers while leaning on a converted classic Chevrolet car, Havana, Cuba, 2019.

initiatives and the inefficiencies of centralized economic planning.

Cubans have a saying, 'Es un arroz con mango,' meaning, 'It's rice with mango,' or 'It's complicated,' or, more than complicated, 'It's completely bollixed up.' In stronger American slang, 'It's a cluster****.' Sugar was once the driver of the entire Cuban economy, critical to its rum production, and an important source of foreign exchange and employment, but sugarcane production in 2022 was the lowest since 1908. Cubans might describe their economic problems as outrageous or unbelievable, using the expression, 'le zumba el mango' – or 'to fling a mango'.[11]

Beyond their nutritional value in times of crises, mangoes are much adored throughout Cuba. In Witold Szabłowski's book *How to Feed a Dictator*, the chef Erasmo Hernández describes his preparation of fish in mango sauce for the revolutionary hero Fidel Castro.[12] Well-known varieties in Cuba today include the sweet, yellow Bizcochuelo mango from the El Caney province of Santiago de Cuba, made famous by popular musicians such as salsa singer Celia Cruz with her song 'Mango Mangüe', which is reminiscent of the calls of the *pregoneros*, street-food vendors selling their wares.

Haiti, the poorest country in the Western Hemisphere, is rich in mangoes, its national fruit. Mangoes are one of Haiti's most important export crops. However, in recent years, the country is losing its share of the large and growing U.S. market to Mexico, Brazil, Peru, Ecuador and Guatemala. Until recent political instability in the country, U.S. grocery retailer Whole Foods was the sole buyer of Certified Organic mangoes from small Haitian growers as part of their Whole Foods Fair Trade programme.

While numerous varieties of mangoes can be found in Haiti, the most famous is the Francine (also called Madame Francis, Francique or Fransik). The origin of the name of this

Willy Jean Paul, *Haitian Market Women*, 2021, watercolour.

mango is unknown, but Louise King, director of tropical fruits at the Fruit and Spice Park in Homestead, Florida, suggests that, like the names of many other mango varieties, it may have derived from the owner of the orchard where the mango was first grown. This mango is able to withstand the hot water treatment required to kill fly larvae of the Mediterranean fruit fly and thus can be exported.

Jamaicans have a saying during mango season on the island: 'Turn down the pots!' With mangoes freely available for the picking, no one needs to cook; mangoes make the meal.[13] Number 11 and Julie are two popular Jamaican varieties, but sources list more than 65 colourful mango names, including John Bellyfull, Hairy, Sweetie Come Brush Me, Roadie and Back of Kitchen.[14] In a sea battle with the French in 1782, the victorious British Captain Lord Rodney confiscated a cargo of plants including mangoes which was en route from Mauritius to Haiti. Rodney redirected them to Jamaica, where they flourished in newly established botanic gardens.[15] The plants had been packed for shipping in wooden crates labelled with 'No. 11', and the varietal retains that name today.[16]

Once a major player in the sugar trade, the tiny island of Nevis and its partner, St Kitts, lay claim to the title 'Mango Capital of the Caribbean'. The country hosts an annual mango festival that draws international attention to the more than forty types of mangoes available, and innovative mango-focused dishes are showcased by competitive chefs. All Nevisians have at least one mango tree in their back garden, and mango trees grow wild on the roadsides. The country is said to have more monkeys than residents, so the lucky animals feast on the ubiquitous fruit. Nevis mangoes cannot be exported because of their susceptibility to the mango seed weevil, and aside from small amounts of mango pulp, local mangoes stay on the island.[17]

Mango is a comfort food in the Caribbean, and the mango season is highly anticipated. Mangoes inspire fierce loyalty among Caribbean residents to their favourite varieties, which are eaten fresh from the trees or made into salsa or tropical cocktails, among other tasty creations.

American Colonies and the United States

In the northern colonies of the New World, George Washington (1732–1799) and Alexander Hamilton (1755/7–1804) were two American Founding Fathers who visited a location where mangoes grow. Hamilton was born on the Caribbean island of Nevis at a time when sugar plantations were being worked by enslaved persons who would likely have had mango trees in their provision gardens. While there are no records of Hamilton referencing mangoes, mangoes were ubiquitous on Nevis, so he undoubtedly ate them.

Washington's interest in exotic flora can likely be traced back to 1751–2, when, at an impressionable nineteen years of age, he made a trip to the island of Barbados. He accompanied his half-brother Lawrence, who was suffering from tuberculosis and had been advised to spend the colder months in the Caribbean for his health. Mangoes were brought to Barbados from the West African Coast in the 1700s by Spanish and Portuguese explorers and would have been growing on the island at the time of Washington's visit, according to *The Natural History of Barbados* by Griffith Hughes, a publication which Washington was likely to have read in preparation for his trip. Washington's travel diary describes enjoying fruits 'both familiar and new' at dinner parties with the wealthy sugar plantation owners who formed the elite on the island.

Some years later, George Washington was serving mango at his own elegant dinners to the elite of the new country. Exotic foods, such as imported Indian pickled mangoes, would have been luxury edibles served as status symbols for the foodies of the American colonies, much like today's truffles and caviar. In the eighteenth century, one's status in the world was often determined by the food on the table. The cherry may be the fruit we most often associate with George Washington, and we cherish the myth of young George cutting down his father's cherry tree. He may have favoured cherry pie, but preserved documents in the Mount Vernon archives prove he also had a fondness for mangoes and personally imported them for his household. An invoice shows that in September 1759, Washington requested that the London-based merchants Robert Cary & Company procure a 'case of pickles to consist of anchovies, capers, olives, salad oil and one bottle of India mangoes'.[18]

The Washingtons were famous for their gracious and lavish hospitality, entertaining thousands of dinner guests, including celebrities such as the Marquis de Lafayette, Thomas Jefferson and Patrick Henry. They presented elegant and impressive displays at their table, including pickle dishes, commensurate with their important status and position. Washington imported condiments, including Indian pickled mangoes, from Asia, the

Persian pickled mango (*torshi anbeh*).

Mediterranean and the West Indies. Martha Washington (1731–1802) was justly proud of her culinary skills, and George his garden, as noted in Stephen McLeod's book, *Dining with the Washingtons*.[19]

A frequent visitor to Mount Vernon and a fellow Founding Father himself, Thomas Jefferson noted, 'On a hot day in Virginia . . . I know of nothing more comforting than a fine spiced pickle.'[20] Pickling is an efficient method for food preservation that has been practised worldwide for centuries, and involves fermentation in brine or immersion in vinegar. In fact, as early as the 1300s, the Moroccan traveller Ibn Battuta noted in his chronicle of daily life in India that preserved mango pickles served as an accompaniment to meals.[21]

Through their culinary experiences in their colonial empire in India, the British developed a taste for Indian mango pickles. The sharp pickled flavours provided interest and contrast to the blander rice dishes. This new trend was then mimicked on the tables of the wealthy and in taverns of the American colonies.

Tropical fruits were introduced into the colonies of the Caribbean islands by the British, French and Spanish, who were searching for possible sites where they might flourish. During Washington's time, exotic foodstuffs like mango began to arrive by ship into the harbour of Philadelphia, the most important port in the colonies. Back then, the only way a fragile fresh mango would have been able to survive the journey from India to either Britain or the American colonies in an edible form was by being preserved, by way of being made into pickles, chutneys and jams. The Mount Vernon gift shop today proudly features 'habanero peach mango' preserves, which are made in the tradition of eighteenth-century food preservation techniques. The Ploughman's lunch, a favourite pub menu today in Britain, always includes some sort of pickled condiment, such as mango chutney.

Miles away from his plantation in Virginia, and hard at work in Philadelphia establishing a new country, Washington would have regularly been offered mango pickles, relishes and chutneys as staples of colonial tavern fare. The menu at the famed City Tavern in Philadelphia, where Washington regularly dined, featured mango and papaya relish.

While wives in Indian villages were preparing mango pickles according to family recipes passed down for generations, British foodies found interesting workarounds when fresh mangoes for pickling were unavailable or too expensive. In 1717 in England, T. Williams, a cook at the London Crown and Anchor Tavern, included instructions on how 'to pickle Codlins like Mango' in his book *The Accomplished Housekeeper, and Universal Cook*. 'Codlin' is a general term for small sour apples grown in Britain that have an elongated shape, somewhat resembling a mango. Likewise, Martha Washington supplemented the expensive gourmet provisions of bottled, preserved mangoes imported by her husband from India by making her own 'India pickles'. Her pickles were not made from mangoes, which grow only in tropical climates, but were made from Washington's cherries, green peppers and home-grown musk melons from her garden at Mount Vernon. Green peppers even came to be called 'mangoes', the word 'mango' evolving into a verb meaning 'to pickle'. There are instructions in what has been called the first American cookbook, *American Cookery*, published by Amelia Simmons in 1796, on how 'to pickle or make mangoes of melons'. Today in the American Midwest green peppers are often still referred to as 'mangoes' or 'mango peppers'. Another cookbook known to be in Martha's possession, the 1765 edition of *The Art of Cookery, Made Plain and Easy* by Hannah Glasse, gives detailed instructions on how to make India pickle or *paco-lilla* – from which English piccalilli, widely available in the UK today, comes from. *Paco-lilla*, according to Glasse, is made 'the same [way] the mangoes come over in', but using the spice long pepper and cabbage instead of mango.

Special decorative dishes, 'pickle plates', were used to serve pickles in the Washington household. Six pickle plates were listed on documents as purchased by George Washington at an auction in 1774, and there are pickle plates in the collection at Mount Vernon. Twenty-seven 'pickle pots' were found in the cellar of the mansion upon Washington's death.

Mango may be the only fruit that has a specific fork designed to make eating this messy fruit a bit more manageable. The fork is three-pronged, with a longer, sharp middle tine to insert into the mango. In the 1800s the Dutch designed mango forks with elaborate silver patterns. Mango forks are still produced and used in Mexico today. No doubt if they had been available, they would have been on Martha Washington's elegant table.

In 1798, while Martha was making and serving pickles, George Washington was adjusting to his retirement from the U.S. presidency following the inauguration of John Adams and anxious to return to gardening at Mount Vernon. He purchased, collected and shared seeds with fellow plant-lovers hoping to learn what might be viable to grow in the newly independent nation. Like Thomas Jefferson, Washington was an avid gardener who sought to expand the types of foodstuffs available in the fledgling country of the United States. His detailed records show he ordered seeds for 'exotic' plants, including mango seeds, and experimented with germinating them in his personally designed, temperature-controlled greenhouse. However, while visitors to Mount Vernon and Jefferson's Monticello remarked on the stunning fruits of the lemon and orange trees, there are no mentions of mango fruits. Although they may grow leaves, mango trees do not easily bear fruit in greenhouses – difficult, but not impossible, for in the 1790s Henry Pratt, a wealthy colonial shipping merchant who developed Lemon Hill, an extensive garden and greenhouse outside of Philadelphia, was awarded a prize by the Pennsylvania Horticultural Society for exhibiting the first mango fruit grown from a mango tree in a greenhouse in the United States. Fruiting mango trees are noted in an 1809 journal entry of a visitor to the Woodlands, another renowned colonial garden and greenhouse, designed by Richard Hamilton (no relation to Alexander), located on the Delaware River north of Philadelphia.[22] George Washington had high praise for a North American native fruit, the pawpaw, which has been described as having the flavour of tropical fruits like mangoes and bananas, and, though not related to the *Mangifera indica*, it is sometimes referred to as the 'Hillbilly mango'.

In 1898, on the cusp of the twentieth century, the U.S. government became serious about the search for new plant species that could be viable to grow domestically. The Office of Seed and Plant Introduction was founded under the auspices of the United States Department of Agriculture (USDA) with the same goal of searching the world for plants that could increase commercial agriculture at home and reduce the country's economic reliance on imported food products.

Heading up this office was a dream job for its determined creator and first appointee, David Fairchild (1869–1954), a 22-year-old botanist from Kansas who had a major case of wanderlust. Fairchild had the extraordinary good fortune of attracting the attention and then lasting friendship of a fellow plant-hunter, Barbour Lathrop (1847–1927), who also happened to have the personal resources sufficient to support their ambitious worldwide plant-collecting adventures. Mango was a favourite fruit of Fairchild's, second only to mangosteen (which is not related to mango). During the four years in which he travelled on his own and with Lathrop, Fairfield sent back to the USDA 24 varieties of mangoes from six countries.[23]

A fellow Kansan, the horticulture professor and colleague of Fairchild's Elbridge Gale (1825–1907), also played an important part in the introduction of mango cultivation in the United States. On the grounds of his retirement home, aptly named Mangonia, Gale planted several grafted saplings that had been forwarded to him from Pune, India. He named the resulting variety 'Mulgoba'. Seeds of the Mulgoba were purchased by another retired couple, Captain John Haden (1853–1903) and his wife Florence (1860–1949). Their combination of the Mulgoba with the fibrous, strong-smelling Turpentine mango that had made its way from the lowlands of the Caribbean islands proved fortuitous. By the time those seedlings produced fruits, Captain Haden had passed away, but his wife named the

David Fairchild (1869–1954).

truly beautiful variety the 'Haden' after her husband. She also marketed the fruit in Florida and developed her own mango chutney recipe. One hundred years later, seedlings from the Haden produced the Kent, Keitt and Tommy Atkins mangoes, which are among the most profitable commercial varieties in the world.[24]

When he retired to Miami, Florida, in 1938, Fairchild and a group of supporters created Fairchild Garden, a unique public botanical garden of tropical plants, which includes facilities for research and education. Numerous specimens collected by Fairchild remain in the garden today, and it is renowned for its annual mango festival. One such variety, the Fairchild, named in honour of David Fairchild, has a complicated history of 'movement' – originating in the Panama Canal Zone in the 1900s, it

Fruiting mango tree, Homestead, Florida.

Deborah Griscom Passmore, *Mulgoba Mango*, 1907, watercolour
illustration for the USDA Pomological Watercolor Collection.

was brought to the United States through Hawaii in 1926, and introduced by David Fairchild to Florida in 1938. It was subsequently lost and then reintroduced in 1992, when it was brought back to the Fairchild Garden in Florida from Honduras.

Between the years 1899 and 1937, 528 varieties of mangoes from India, the Philippines, the West Indies and other countries were introduced to the United States by the USDA. Not only did the USDA set about collecting fruits, including mangoes, but prior to colour photography, the department enlisted artists to document them accurately. There are 7,584 paintings in the USDA Pomological Watercolor Collection today, including eighty renditions of mangoes.

The USDA Germplasm repository, established in 1898, houses samples of several hundred mango varietals and is the location of continued research on improved mango selection and cultivation. In an interesting twist of fate, the repository in Florida serves as a source for the reverse flow of varieties originally sourced from other parts of the world.

The 1970s was a glorious decade for mango cultivation in Florida. Today 99 per cent of the mangoes in the U.S. market come from Mexico, Central America, Ecuador and Brazil, but they all had their ancestral roots in Florida. Perfecting the mango continues to be an obsession for the Zill family in southern Florida. In 1940 horticulturalist and nursery owner Lawrence Zill began propagating a cultivar named after his family, the Zill mango, derived from the Florida Haden, which is planted commercially and widely used as nursery stock. Subsequent new mangoes evolving from this mango are named after other family members: Carrie, Dot and Gary. In the 1990s Lawrence's son Gary, also a nurseryman, began an ambitious Mango Variety and Selection Development Project, planting over 10,000 seedlings based on the aroma of the leaves and sap as an indicator of the flavour of the mango that would grow from a cutting.

Twenty to thirty superior varieties were selected specifically for their aroma, including Sugar Loaf, Fruit Punch, Harvest Moon, Coconut Cream, Fruit Cocktail, Ugly Betty, Pineapple Pleasure and Venus.[25]

In 1991 a group of chefs in the Miami area, naming themselves the 'Mango Gang', decided to work collaboratively to celebrate and publicize the unique cuisine of southern Florida. The mango became the perfect icon, both exotic and local. Norman van Aken, Allen Susser, Douglas Rodriguez and Mark Militello highlighted the use of local tropical and subtropical ingredients and the influences of local Caribbean and South American populations in each of their individual restaurants. The chefs are still very much a part of the Miami food scene that they helped to create thirty years ago. Home chefs continue to enjoy participating in annual mango festival baking competitions on Pine Island, Florida.

As more and more South Asians come to reside in the United States and more Americans are exposed to excellent South Asian mangoes in their travels, there is an increasing demand for those mango varieties. Due to the short (six- to eight-week) growing season and the very high cost of transportation and export/import requirements, few South Asian mangoes make it to the U.S. market. One of the few importers of Indian mangoes to the United States, Bhaskar Savani, a Gujarati-born dentist now living in the United States, is dedicated to helping fulfil this need, working towards eliminating import restrictions and bringing prized Alphonsos and Kesars by plane to the U.S. market from his family farm in India. Savani combines his passion for his Indian home-grown mangoes with unique wildlife conservation efforts, encouraging farmers in India to plant mango trees that will establish agro-corridors for wild animals, including endangered Asiatic lions, helping to connect already established national parks.[26]

In the footsteps of David Fairchild, contemporary fruit-hunters Richard Campbell and Noris Ledesma conducted research at Fairchild Garden for many years. Today both continue to search the world for the perfect mango variety for the U.S. market. Campbell is a consultant with the Ciruli Brothers, who have successfully rebranded the Mexican Ataulfo mango as the Champagne Mango, weaning the American consumers away from their obsession with equating the colour red with ripeness. Ciruli Brothers grow mangoes all the way up the Pacific Coast of Mexico, harvesting locally as the fruit ripens, thus extending the season. Ledesma is developing a lovely deep-purple-coloured mango, which will camouflage slight imperfections from fussy consumers and still deliver the desired flavour.

3
Mughals and Mangoes

Some twelve hundred years before the Mughals, Ashoka the Great (268 BCE–232 BCE), the beloved Indian ruler during the thriving Mauryan Empire (321 BCE–185 BCE), converted to Buddhism, renounced violence and turned his back on war following bloody battles he had fought on the way to creating his empire. He erected huge inscribed edict pillars throughout the empire, proclaiming his gift of planting mango groves along travel routes to provide sustenance for the poor and hungry. Today Ashoka is the name of a leading ready-to-eat food brand in India, whose products include Alphonso and Kesar mango pulp, mango pickles, chutneys and more modern offerings such as Tango Mango dipping sauce. Founded in Mumbai in the 1930s, the company's mission states, 'We are passionate about feeding the world.'[1] Ashoka is also the name of an organization founded in 1980 to encourage social entrepreneurs 'envisioning a world in which everyone is a changemaker'. It has supported many projects around the world, including a number of initiatives that help mango growers.[2]

Emperor Harshavardhana (c. 590–647 CE), known as Harsha, was another important Indian emperor who ruled the northern part of the country from 606 to 647 CE, three hundred years after the empire of Ashoka and still nine hundred years before the Mughals. Chronicles of his time catalogue

Ashoka edict pillar, Bihar, India.

tributes sent to him that included jewels, silks, precious stones, gold, silver, woven baskets, spices, exotic animals, birds and, surprisingly, mango sap, an expensive delicacy described as being packed in thick bamboo tubes.[3] A visiting Chinese Monk, Hiuen Tsang (602–664 CE), describes the famous Buddhist university, Nalanda, during Harsha's rule as having 'groves of mango trees that offer the inhabitants their dense and protective shade'.[4] He noted that mangoes are grown throughout India.

But it was the extravagant Mughal rulers who were avid horticulturalists and left us detailed records of their mango love. Written records and personal journals document that each of the Mughal emperors, from Babur to Humayan, Akbar, Jahangir, Shah Jahan, Aurangzeb and finally the last Mughal ruler, Zafar, enjoyed mangoes and took a keen interest in the cultivation of this native South Asian fruit.

Did mangoes play a part in establishing the first Mughal Empire? Sources suggest that Babur (1483–1530), an avid fruit-loving ruler in Samarkand, was convinced to become involved in the politics of India by Daulat Khan Lodi, who promised him territory and war booty. But it may have been a strategic gift of mangoes that ultimately won Babur's support. Babur defeated Lodi's enemy Rana Sanga of Mewar (*c.* 1482–1528), thus establishing the foundations of the Mughal Empire.[5]

During his reign in the sixteenth century, Emperor Babur kept detailed notes of his daily life and surroundings in the *Baburnama* (1525–6), considered to be the first autobiography in Muslim literature. Babur's grandsons later had this manu-script illustrated and included his thoughts on the mango, especially his preference for musk melon from his native Persia: 'Mangoes when good, are very good. They are usually plucked unripe and ripened in the house. Unripe, they make excellent condiments, are also good preserved in syrup. Taking it altogether, the mango is the best fruit of Hindustan.'[6] Babur describes in detail two ways of eating mangoes: either squeezing the mango to a pulp, making a hole in it and sucking out the tasty juice, or peeling it as one would a juicy peach.[7]

Babur's grandson Akbar (1542–1605) was a great champion of the mango and promoted mango orchards throughout his empire. It was during his rule that formal orchards were dev-eloped as part of grand Mughal gardens, and he himself initiated the creation of the famous Lal Bagh, an orchard of a thousand mango trees, planted near Darbhanga.[8]

Gardening and horticulture became obsessions for Mughal emperors. Lush fruit trees, including mango trees, provide the additional benefit of dense shade. William Dalrymple, author of *The Last Mughal* (2006), notes that 'For the Mughals,

Mango tree, miniature painting from the
Baburnama (Memoirs of Babur), *c.* 1590.

Alphonso mangoes on display at a market in Singapore.

gardens were regarded as reflections of paradise and a connoisseurship of plants and scents was considered a central attribute of a civilized mind.'[9]

Mangoes are mentioned numerous times in the sixteenth-century record *Ain-i-Akbari*, compiled on Akbar's orders by Abul Fazl (1551–1602), his court scribe. Describing the flora of Akbar's kingdom, Abul Fazl notes that the mango is 'unrivaled in colour, smell, and taste', surpassing even the much-prized musk melons and grapes of the original homeland of the Mughal rulers.

> In shape, it resembles an apricot, or a quince, or a pear, or a melon, and weighs even one ser [approx. 1 litre in dry volume, or 1 kilogram] and upwards. There are green, yellow, red, variegated, sweet, and subacid mangoes. Tho the tree looks well, especially when young; it is larger than a nut tree, and its leaves resemble those of the willow but are larger. The new leaves appear soon after the fall of the old ones in autumn and look green and yellow, orange, peach-coloured, and bright red. The flower which opens in spring

resembles that of the vine, has a good smell, and looks very curious.[10]

Abul Fazl recounts that mangoes are to be found everywhere in India, due, in part, to the stewardship of His Majesty, Akbar, and notes the uses of the unripe sour green fruit for making preserves and pickles. He describes an unusual fertilizing practice of putting milk and treacle around the tree, intended to make the fruits sweeter, and cautions that the fruit production of a mango tree can vary greatly from year to year, from a rich harvest to no fruit at all.[11]

Details about medicinal uses of the mango are documented, as well as harvesting and preservation techniques:

> When people eat a great deal of mangoes, they may promote digestion by partaking of milk with the kernels of the mango stones. The kernels of old stones are subacid and taste well. When two or three years old, they are used as medicine. If a half-ripe mango, together with its stalk to a length of about two fingers, be taken from the tree, and the broken end of its stalk be closed with warm wax, and kept in butter, or honey, the fruit will retain its taste for two or three months, whilst the colour will remain even for a year.[12]

Carrying on the tradition of mango adoration, Jahangir (1569–1627), son and successor of Akbar, states specifically that of all the fine fruits of his empire, he was fondest of the mango.[13] In *Tuzuk of Jahangir*, the memoirs of Jahangir, he makes comparative notes and declares that in the sweetness of its juice, fragrance, flavour and digestibility, the mangoes of Chapramau, in the province of Agra, are superior to all mangoes. As an encouragement for his subjects to pursue the unpredictable,

Jahangir welcoming Shah Abbas, Mughal School, *c.* 1620, watercolour, gold and ink on paper.

expensive and labour-intensive practice of fruit production, Emperor Jahangir did not tax gardeners.[14]

Noorjahan (*c.* 1577–1645) was the favourite wife of Jahangir, and she exerted great influence over her husband, who was addicted to opium. She favoured mango drinks and created wines flavoured with mango and roses. A rare mango, named Noorjahan after this Mughal queen, is cultivated only in the

Wine flavoured with mango and rose, an adaptation of Noorjahan's Mughal recipe.

Katthiwada in Madhya Pradesh. Today mango aficionados reserve their Noorjahan mangoes, which can grow up to 30 centimetres (1 ft) in length, weeks before they are harvested. As recently as five years ago, this mango was on the verge of extinction, but efforts by the local state government to encourage its cultivation have been successful.[15] Another Mughal lady immortalized by a mango variety is the dancer and courtesan Anarkali, whose story is a popular theme for Bollywood. This mango is unique in that the pulp of each side when sliced open has a distinctly different colour, aroma and flavour.[16]

The patronage of the Mughal emperors advanced experiments in horticulture, especially in grafting, which resulted in thousands of new mango varieties, including the famous Totapuri, or Bangalore. Its name literally translates to 'parrot beak', referring to the pointed end of this mango variety, one of the main cultivars grown in India. The skin is less bitter than other varieties and is sometimes consumed with the flesh itself. The Jahangir mango, named in honour of this emperor, is a much-prized mango variety today.[17]

Just as Mughal leaders were immortalized with their individual mango varieties, contemporary political figures and even sports personalities and actresses have mango varieties named after them. NaMo mango was named for Indian prime minister Narendra Modi in 2015. Two existing varieties of mango were combined in 2010 to create the Sachin, named after Sachin Tendulkar, a star of India's national cricket team who retired from Test matches in 2013. The Aishwarya Rai mango was named for the famous actress and model, who was voted Miss World in 1994.

Though grafting as a propagation technique had been known as early as the fourth century from descriptions of the 'Sixty-Four Arts' in the *Kama Sutra*, the practice had been allowed only in the royal gardens. Shah Jahan, son of Jahangir, lifted the ban.[18] Skill in grafting mangoes is much celebrated in South Asia even today. Mango growers in India and worldwide are experimenting with novel ways to increase success and productivity in grafting techniques, including grafting seedlings in plastic bags and using banana hormones.

In addition to enjoying the sight, smell and taste of fresh-picked mangoes, Jahangir and Shah Jahan rewarded their personal court chefs, known as *Khansamahs*, for inventing uniquely prepared dishes using the fruit. Some of these complex dishes are still prepared today for special occasions, including *aam panna*, a drink made of sour, unripe mangoes, and *aam ka meetha pulao* or *amba pulao*, a popular rice and mango dish. Mughal dining was not a simple matter, and large numbers of dishes were served at each meal – events which could go on for hours. Food was cooked in pure rainwater that was mixed with precious water carried all the way from the sacred Ganges River. It was served on gold and silver dishes embellished with precious stones and jade, which was thought to have the ability to detect poison.[19]

Instructions for creating elaborate mango culinary dishes, medicinal preparations and aphrodisiacs are described in the *Ni'matnama of the Sultans of Mandu* (The Sultan's Book of Delights), collected and illustrated in the late fifteenth century. Examples include recipes for both sweet and savoury dishes, methods for curing gastric ailments and impotence, as well as instructions for preparing perfumes. Even before Mughal times, a famous feast held by Alauddin Khalji (1296–1316) at the Savima Fort was composed of all mango dishes. Khalji reportedly announced that mango was his personal aphrodisiac.[20]

As the previous Mughal rulers had, Shah Jahan loved fresh fruits, particularly mangoes, and is known to have punished his own son Aurangzeb for hoarding mangoes from one of his favourite trees in the Deccan instead of forwarding them to his

Women enjoying the river by a mango tree, Mughal School, *c.* 1765, tempera and gold on paper.

Mango festival, New Delhi, 2018.

father's court.[21] During Aurangzeb's rule, Niccolao Manucci (1638–1717), the Venetian explorer and author of the *Storia do Mogor*, documented what he observed in Brampur (Burhanpur): 'In this town there is plenty of fruit, such as amb (ambah) or mungiis mango – the best fruit to be found in India.'[22]

Mughal rulers were mango-lovers to the very end of their empire. Mughal Bahadur Shah II, known by the pen name Zafar, spent his evenings 'enjoying the moonlight, listening to singers or eating fresh mangoes', according to William Dalrymple.[23] Zafar was exiled by the British to Myanmar, where the old man quietly passed away.

Horticultural archaeology determined that mango trees once thrived in the gardens surrounding the most renowned example of Mughal architecture, the Taj Mahal, which was commissioned by Shah Jahan for his true love, Mumtaz Mahal. The plantings that are there today are a legacy of the British rule of Lord Curzon, whose idea of restoring the garden in 1909 involved removing original trees to create a flat vista.[24] We can get a glimpse of what the stunning Mughal gardens would have looked like by visiting the restored Pinjore Gardens, built as a summer retreat for Aurangzeb (1618–1707) at the time he relocated his capital to Lahore. The Pinjore Mango Mela is an annual festival held in these gardens, at which mango products are featured and mango-eating competitions are keenly anticipated.

Giving gifts and bestowing honours were important features of Mughal court ritual, as they helped to establish that the ruler was the source of all wealth; the recipient, in accepting of his leader's beneficence, acknowledged his own submissive position. From the sixteenth to the nineteenth century, the Mughal rulers were masters of mango diplomacy, but the tradition of gifting both the trees and the fruit had existed for centuries before their time. Mangoes are a 'hell of a fruit', U.S. President George W. Bush proclaimed when he was served mangoes in India on a diplomatic visit in 2006. He was participating in an ancient food-gifting tradition involving this fruit in South Asia. The gift of mangoes was, in reality, a trade negotiation with provisions that included removing the import ban on American company Harley Davidson. In return, Indian mangoes would come to the United States for the first time since 1989, when a prohibition had been placed on the fruit because of pest infestation concerns.[25]

To this day, as in the time of the Mughals, diplomatic gifts of mangoes are exchanged for numerous reasons and with many goals in mind. The finest-quality mangoes are passed between the leaders of India and Pakistan annually, even in times of tense diplomatic relations. The Pakistani Foreign Office released this statement in 2021: 'Every year, the president of Pakistan sends high-quality mangoes as a gift to selected countries as part of goodwill and to promote our trade diplomacy.'[26]

Queen Victoria and Abdul Karim, Balmoral, October 1895, gelatin silver print.

4

The British and European Connection to Mango

'What is a mango?', actress Dame Judi Dench, in the role of Queen Victoria, asks actor Ali Fazal, playing the part of Abdul Karim, a young Indian clerk who becomes a close confidant of the Queen, in the 2017 film *Victoria and Abdul*. 'It is the queen of fruits, your majesty,' he proclaims. But when a sample of the amazing fruit is sent for and arrives after the six-week-long voyage from India, it has clearly gone 'off'.

Biographer Shrabani Basa, author of *Victoria and Abdul: The True Story of the Queen's Closest Confidant* (2010), confirms the accuracy of this incident. Queen Victoria, who also held the title Empress of India, likely never tasted a fresh mango. However, she did learn to enjoy Indian foods, including curries, pickles and chutneys, from her friendship with Abdul and even had them prepared daily on the palace menu. In a touching foodie parallel, Fazal, a great mango fan, sent a gift of fresh Alphonso mangoes to Judi Dench, his real-life 'queen' and acting mentor.[1]

In 2017, while he was the executive chef at Junoon in New York City, Michelin-starred Indian chef Vikas Khanna created a mango dessert inspired by this scene to celebrate the launch of the film. Khanna was awarded the title of New York's Hottest

Chef by *Eater New York* two years in a row, 2011 and 2012. Khanna, along with Hari Nayak, has written the cookbook *Mango Mia: Celebrating the Tropical World of Mangoes*.

Eight-tiered dessert stands that featured moulded-fruit wreath decorations were part of a 56-piece porcelain dessert set made by Rockingham Works now in the Royal Collection Trust, which was used in the 1838 coronation of Queen Victoria. The East and West Indian fruit decorations, which include mangoes, are identified by inscriptions under each as a celebration of the vastness of the British Empire, of which the queen was so proud. Another charming gift in the Royal Collection is

Mango forks.

a delicately carved scene of a toran, or temple arch, surrounded by an Indian village scene that includes mango trees in fruit. This vignette was presented to Queen Elizabeth II by the governor of Gujarat in 1961, the year she made a Commonwealth visit to India.

Queen Victoria was a great champion of etiquette and elaborate table manners and would likely not have approved of the messiness of eating a mango, since the juiciest ones defy cutlery. During her reign, cutlery expanded worldwide as the British established the standard for 'civilized' table manners in their vast colonial empire. Many mango-lovers, such as Nadine Thompson-Barham, owner of the Grand Mango Caribbean Restaurant in Central Valley, New York, insist that using a knife and fork 'defeats the purpose of eating a mango', though during the Victorian period a mango fork was designed.

M. S. Randhawa (1909–1986) was a renowned Punjabi government administrator during the twentieth century and had a long career as a historian, botanist and landscape designer, notably of the garden city of Chandigarh. Of mangoes, Randhawa wrote, 'The British did not savor the sight of Indians squatting on the floor and sucking on mangoes, with the juice flowing down their elbows. They often referred to it as the "bathroom fruit," and instructed their Indian servants to confine the mess of mango eating to the bathroom.'[2] For his work in arboriculture, Randhawa is honoured in India to this day with an annual art and literature festival. In July 2019, a mango-sucking festival, Amb-Choop Mela, was held in Kala Bagh in his honour.[3] Author of *Flowering Trees in India*, Randhawa related stories about traditional horticulture: 'How young I was when I planted the mango and still the leaves are full of life. But there is none in my old body.' Randhawa quotes Verrier Elwin (1902–1964), a British-born Indian anthropologist: 'The old man who planted mango and tamarind trees in his youth finds himself jealous of the vigour of their fresh green leaves and contrasts it with the lack of strength in his own limbs.'[4]

British settlers in India under the British Raj may not have eaten fresh mangoes with their hands, but they did develop a taste for preserved mangoes in the form of chutneys. Though the details were never documented, Major Grey's Chutney was reputedly created by a nineteenth-century British Army officer who served in British India. A mild condiment available widely in the United States from several manufacturers, its ingredients include mango, raisins, vinegar, lime juice, onion, tamarind extract, sweeteners and various spices. Chutneys are an essential element of the 'Ploughman's lunch', an English cold meal based on bread, cheese and sweet/sour condiments, originally conceived for workmen to take out into the fields.

Intrepid Victorian women wrote about their encounters with the mango in locations where it grows. Botanical explorer, artist and worldwide traveller Marianne North documented the mango tree, its flowers and its fruit in several of her paintings, including one created in India in the 1870s titled *Foliage and Flowers of the Clove, Fruit of the Mango and Hindoo God of Wisdom*. She presented more than nine hundred works of art to the Royal Botanic Gardens, Kew, in the 1880s. In her notes, she writes, 'The Mango (*Mangifera indica L.*) is generally regarded as one of the most delicious tropical fruits, though there are many varieties, differing very much in quality. In an unripe state the fruit is much used in tarts and preserved in sugar or vinegar.'[5]

Lady Annie Brassey (1839–1887) was a widely read Victorian author who travelled the world with her husband, five children and their dog on board their luxury yacht. In her published travel notes, *A Voyage in the 'Sunbeam': Our Home on the Ocean for Eleven Months* (1878), she described the first day she tasted mangoes:

Ploughman's lunch with Major Grey's mango chutney.

the King of Fruits – a combination of Apricot and Pine apple, and the best sorts certainly have a subtle blending of many agreeable flavours, but the common seedling tree bears fruit in which a mixture of turpentine, and treacle is usually prominent, and of the sorts that are greatly valued by those who have lived with them from childhood are very disagreeable to strangers. The best sorts are without fibre in the pulp, and are eaten with a spoon, like custard, but some fibrous sorts are celebrated for delicious piquant flavour and are eaten by sucking the pulp pressed out through a hole in the skin.[6]

She further writes,

To enjoy mangoes thoroughly you ought not to eat them in company, but leaning over the side of the ship in the early morning, with your sleeves tucked up to your elbows,

Marianne North, *Mango and Ganesha*, 1870s, oil on board.

using no knife and fork, but tearing off the skin with your teeth and sucking the abundant juice.[7]

Lady Maria Callcott (1785–1842) was the daughter of a naval officer who lived and travelled widely in India and Ceylon (Sri Lanka). In her *Journal of a Residence in India*, published in 1812, she describes Mazagong's (a section of today's Indian city of Mumbai) fame as due to the mangoes grown there, 'certainly the best fruit I ever tasted'. She noted,

the parent tree, from which all those of this species have been grafted, is honoured during the fruit season by a guard of sepoys; and in the reign of Shah Jahan, couriers were stationed between Delhi and Mahratta coast to secure an abundant and fresh supply of mangoes for the royal table.[8]

Mango tree near Pune, India, 1895.

Isabella Lucy Bird (1831–1904) authored numerous books of her travels and observations, including *The Golden Chersonese and the Way Thither* (1883) about adventures in the Malay Peninsula. An explorer, photographer and naturalist, she was the first woman to be elected Fellow of the Royal Geographical Society. She describes her experience with mangoes in the Hawaiian Islands:

> Mr. K., from whose house we started, has the finest mango grove on the islands. It is a fine foliaged tree, but is everywhere covered with a black blight, which gives the groves the appearance of being in mourning, as the tough, glutinous film covers all the older leaves. The mango is an exotic fruit, and people think a great deal of it, and send boxes of mangoes as presents to their friends. It is yellow, with a reddish bloom, something like a magnum bonum plum, three times magnified. The only way of eating it in comfort is to have a tub of water beside you. It should be eaten in private by anyone who wants to retain the admiration of his friends. It has an immense stone, and a disproportionately small pulp. I think it tastes strongly of turpentine at first, but this is a heresy.[9]

With a few exceptions, mangoes cannot be grown in the British Isles or almost anywhere in Continental Europe except in small micro-climates along the southern coast of Spain near Málaga and in Sicily. Farmers have been replacing olive groves with more profitable mango trees, though this is proving to be controversial. The additional water required for fruit production in the Mediterranean climate is changing the balance of resources.

Climate change is allowing the cultivation of mangoes as a speciality product in a very limited area on the island of Sicily.

Sicilian farmers have successfully cultivated lemons and oranges for centuries, but these traditional fruits now must compete with cheaper imports. Because the climate of the island has risen 1.5°C (2.7°F) in the last one hundred years, tropical fruits, particularly mangoes, have become a viable option for the local economy.[10]

While mangoes are not widely cultivated commercially in Europe or in the USA, the flavour of mango is becoming more and more popular. Technical improvements in transport systems increasingly allow the successful importation of the fruit from mango-producing countries year round, including from Burkina Faso, Ivory Coast and Mali, as well as Brazil, Peru, Dominican Republic and Mexico.

Traditional French haute cuisine, which prioritizes local, fresh and seasonal products, is making room for the 'exotic' flavour of mango. Renowned French pastry chef Pierre Hermé, known as the 'Picasso of Pastry', created a confiture from the popular combination of mango and passion fruit, as well as a mango macaron and a mango tart with coconut cream. Cédric Grolet, winner of the title of the World's Best Pastry Chef in 2018, focuses on creating desserts that are *trompe l'oeil* sculptures of fruit, including mangoes. This innovative French pastry chef at the Hotel Meurice in Paris reinterprets traditional French desserts, and his stunning Rubik's Cube cake includes chocolate, chilli and mango cake squares.

Michelin-starred restaurants in Europe often conclude their menus with elaborate mango desserts, at once familiar and exotic, including the pairing of mango with chocolate. The combination of dark chocolate, mango and lemongrass results in a delightful confection offered at the family-owned chocolate firm Butlers in Ireland. Hotel Chocolat, a British chocolatier and cocoa grower, and the only company in the United Kingdom to grow cocoa on its own farm, sells dark-chocolate

A mango-shaped dessert with mango flavouring, A La Mousse restaurant, Philadelphia.

'enrobed' mango pieces and a confection called 'mango smoothie' made with mango, whipping cream and white chocolate.

Hotel Chocolat also produces a mango and passion fruit gin liqueur. Mongozo Mango beer is a fruit beer described on its website as the first organic, gluten-free and fair-trade beer worldwide using sustainable production processes. Galway Spirits Distillery in Galway, Ireland, markets mango-flavoured vodka, declaring, 'The gift of mangoes is considered a gesture of friendship, so share this vodka over ice with friends.'[11]

Some of the best-known and finest-quality commercial mango purée producers are French companies, for example CapFruit, La Fruitière and Boiron. Mango juice is just as likely as orange juice to appear as a breakfast option along with a croissant in a French hotel. Delightful, intensely flavoured mango *pâte de fruit* (fruit jelly sweet) is produced in French *confiseries* (confectioners).

While Spanish mangoes are only available from Málaga in August, mangoes from Africa and South America are widely available in French and Spanish markets virtually year-round, and unusual products such as mango salt and flavoured dried mango are on offer. British mango growers Sally and Denis Pead, who have lived in Málaga for more than twenty years, remark that it takes some coaxing to move the traditional Spanish Mediterranean diet towards a new flavour like mango chutney, though the taste is spectacular with traditional Spanish cheeses. Mango orchard farmers Stephanie Guillou and Giuseppe Forenze find the same reluctance to experiment with mango as a food or flavour with the general public in Sicily, while speciality bars appreciate the options for new cocktails.

Mango French *confiserie*, Paris.

Queen Elizabeth II picks up a mango at a market in the British Virgin Islands, 1977.

Although Queen Victoria may never have had her mango cravings fulfilled, Elizabeth II, according to her former chef John Higgins, 'really enjoyed mangoes. She could tell you how many mangoes were in the fridge at Buckingham Palace.'[12] Mangoes were also among the favourite fruits of the late Queen Mother. Darren McGrady, Kensington Palace chef, in his memoir *Eating Royally: Recipes and Remembrances from a Palace Kitchen* relates a mango tale about Princess Diana:

Along with her caring ways, Diana packed a mischievous sense of humor. She once told a Saudi prince that she liked mangoes after listening to him go on endlessly about the wonderful mangoes in his country. A week later, Diana struggled to carry a huge box of mangoes into the kitchen. She said: 'Do you believe this, Darren? The man sent me a whole crate of mangoes because I mentioned that I liked them. Next time, I need to mention how much I like diamonds.'[13]

Mango lassi drink.

The Buckingham Palace list of gifts received by members of the royal family revealed that Prince Andrew is known to be fond of mangoes, and Princess Anne received a box of one hundred from Mamnoon Hussain, president of Pakistan from 2013 to 2018.[14]

We may think of the wildly popular and ubiquitous mango fruit smoothie as a recent phenomenon made possible by the easy availability of the modern electric blender invented by the Waring company in the 1930s. But in reality, the traditional Indian lassi, made with yoghurt and cardamom and often with mango, pre-dates the blender by several thousand years. While not every smoothie today includes yoghurt, palaeo-ethnobotanists conclude that the fermented milk drink served the purpose of easing digestion. Today it might be difficult to find a smoothie shop anywhere in Europe that does not offer a mango option.

An argument could be made that the mango fruit itself was the first smoothie. Certain mango varieties, known colloquially as 'sucking mangoes', including the Indian Dasheri and the Guatemalan mango de leche are perfect for rolling in one's hand. Vineet Bhatia, formerly head chef of the London restaurant Zaika, instructs, 'You should gently massage the mango like a woman's breast so that the fruit becomes juicy, then peel back the skin and gradually suck the flesh from both the skin and the stone.'[15] Queen Victoria might not approve.

5
Mao, Mangoes
and the East

Presenting prized foods as gifts is an important tradition throughout the world and is especially important in the East. The tradition of gifting mangoes goes back to early Hindu legends, Mughal court traditions and even curious British monarchs, but possibly the most notorious mango 'regift' ever noted took place during Chairman Mao's Cultural Revolution in China. In fact, there is a Chinese term for regifting, *Zhuǎnzèng*, and the practice enhances the status of both the giver and the recipient.[1]

In 1968 Pakistan's foreign minister, Syed Sharifuddin Pirzada, sent a gift of a box of mangoes to Chairman Mao, a common diplomatic gesture of goodwill employed by the politicians of India and Pakistan. Mao, who did not particularly care for mangoes, then passed them on to various factories in China as a reward honouring workers and Red Guard students for their fervent revolutionary spirit and loyalty. Mangoes had been practically unknown in northern China at the time, and these became known as Mao's Golden Mangoes. They were preserved and became treasured icons representing Mao's love for the workers and students, and even representing Mao himself, as reflected in this anonymous poem from the time:

Seeing that golden mango
Was as if seeing the Great Leader Chairman Mao!
Standing before that golden mango
Was just like standing beside Chairman Mao!
Again and again touching the golden mango:
The golden mango was so warm
Again and again smelling the mango:
That golden mango was so fragrant![2]

The Golden Mangoes were proudly taken on tour throughout the country. They were honoured in a series of sacred processions, in many ways mimicking the religious rituals of traditional Buddhism and Daoism, which were forbidden at the time as representing old ways of thinking that must be eliminated. Workers described the strange cult that evolved: 'When one of the mangoes began to rot, workers peeled it and boiled

Mao Zedong mango reliquary, *c.* 1968.

the flesh in a vat of water, which then became "holy" – each worker sipped a spoonful. The mangoes were even placed on an altar to which factory workers would bow.[3] Wax replicas of the mangoes were made and given to revolutionary workers.

The official propaganda department of the Communist Party seized upon the fervour and the theme, manufacturing mango-themed objects of all kinds, from bed sheets to mango-flavoured soaps and cigarettes. This bizarre craze died out after eighteen months. When Imelda Marcos brought a case of mangoes from the Philippines as a gift in 1974, Mao's wife, 'Madame Mao' Jiang Qing, made an unsuccessful attempt to revive the enthusiasm of that first mango cult, even commissioning a film, *Song of the Mango*. In the meantime, Madame Mao was arrested for planning an armed rebellion against the government, and the film was never distributed. The wax models of mangoes were melted down for candles.

The mango cult is not as inexplicable as it might at first seem in the context of how Chinese culture and language makes use of food metaphors. Peaches, for example, are traditionally associated with the Queen Mother of the West, in whose garden mythical long-lived peach trees grew and bore fruit only once in a thousand years, with the fruit symbolizing the wish for a prolonged, healthy life. Because mangoes were an unknown fruit in most of China at this time, they had no previous cultural connection that would be forbidden as 'old thinking', and could be endowed with multiple new meanings. The golden-yellow colour symbolizes the sun, the yang principle, and thus abundance, wealth and happiness. There were rumours that mango trees fruited once a century or even every thousand years, so Mao, having not eaten the mangoes himself, had generously gifted 'immortality' to his loyal followers. Mango souvenirs are collectable even now in Chinese flea markets.[4]

While the mangoes may not have been familiar to the greater part of the Chinese population until as late as the 1960s, the Chinese Buddhist monk Hiuen Tsung had travelled from China to India in the seventh century and had encounters with the fruit and the mango tree. In his journal the monk describes

Chinese mango desserts from Mango Mango Dessert, Philadelphia.

thick mango groves that offered Buddhist pilgrims protective shade. Cultivation of mangoes in the far south of China goes back over 1,000 years, but only in the limited areas where the climate permits. Commercial production of mangoes did not begin until the late 1960s, increasing through the 1980s. In recent years, China has become the second-largest mango producer and the world's largest mango consumer, based on the sheer size of its domestic market.[5]

Hainan Province is the largest producer of mango, followed by Guangxi Autonomous Region, Guangdong Province, Yunnan Province, Sichuan Province and Fujian Province. The mango season in Hainan runs from January to May, in Baise (Guangxi) from June to September and in Panzhihua (Sichuan) from July to November, providing mangoes to the market almost year-round.[6]

The International Mango Symposium was held in Baise in Guangxi Province in 2017, earning the city the title 'Hometown of Mangoes in China'.[7] The oblong, S-shaped variety Guiqi (Guigui), which has green skin and pale-yellow flesh, is cultivated in this area. Its fibreless flesh stores and transports well. The Chinese government has created pilot programmes to combat poverty in this region, encouraging mango production and providing training and financial support to local farmers. The first mango festival in China was held in 2018 in Baise, to promote the varieties of the fruit and products made from mango, including mango wine. A huge sports complex shaped like a mango fruit, popularly known as 'Big Mango', was constructed in Tiandong County, reflecting the pride of the producers in their successful new crop.[8]

Chinese farmers in some areas attach bags to the mangoes as they ripen on the tree to protect them from damage from birds and insects. Some farms have yearly mango tree adoption programmes, in which a subscriber pays to receive all the mangoes on that particular tree, and a monetary contribution is sent to charities. Trees can be inscribed with sentiments: for example, wishes for good luck in university entrance exams.

Chinese markets on the mainland and throughout the diaspora are filled with mango-flavoured snack products, particularly glutinous sweets. Hui Lau Shan is a dessert shop that originated in Hong Kong in the 1960s and began serving fresh mango sweets in 1992. It has now opened locations in the United States. With shops first in New York's Chinatown, Mango Mango Dessert, a Hong Kong-style dessert shop with more than thirty branches worldwide, specializes in fresh mango, drinkable desserts, soups, cakes, teas, crêpes and waffles.

Can mangoes grow in outer space? Experimenting with breeding plants in outer space in 2019, Chinese scientists claim

Shaved ice, Chinese dessert, Singapore.

Chinese mango snacks at a stall in Philadelphia's Chinatown.

to have made a breakthrough. Mango seeds sent aboard a 33-day trip on the Chinese Shenzhou 11 spacecraft were forced to grow in harsh conditions and developed cells that researchers have been able to grow into new tissue. The hope is that mangoes bred in this way may be genetically superior, insect-resistant and of better quality.[9]

Taiwan

One of the most popular fruits in Taiwan, the mango is not a native fruit but was introduced by the Dutch in the seventeenth century. The Taiwan Agricultural Research Institute imported more marketable varieties from the United States in 1954, and

Taiwanese farmers have since developed successful hybrids. The native varietal is known as the Tu mango, which is small, sour and fibrous, often pickled with salt and sugar or made into confectionery.[10] The local weather allows mangoes to be cultivated almost half the year. The Tu mango is sometimes called the 'lovers' fruit' because the sour flavour is associated with troubled romantic relationships.[11]

A hero in the Taiwanese mango world is Cheng Han Chih, 'godfather of mangoes', who took up the challenge of farming the Irwin mango in 1961 and eventually succeeded in growing it and convincing neighbouring farmers to do the same, virtually alleviating poverty in the area. In 1977 Cheng was named among Taiwan's top ten outstanding farmers, and his legacy survives in the orchards tended by his sons and grandsons.[12]

A newcomer in Taiwan is the Xiaxue mango, named because it is as 'rare as the snow in summer'; *xiaxue* means 'snow' and the mango ripens in the summer. It is said to have the intense

Taiwanese mango in the shape of the terraced fields where a decorative herb for the dessert is grown. HoSu restaurant, Taipei, Taiwan.

smell of the Tu mango and is sweeter than other varieties. Farmers are also experimenting with a White mango and a Black Incense mango.[13]

Yujing Mango Festival, also known as the Tainan International Mango Festival, has been held in Taiwan every year since 1999, promoting mango and mango products for the domestic and export market. Creatively using mangoes, HoSu restaurant in Taipei, Taiwan, specializes in local ingredients and features a mango dessert cut to echo the rice paddies of the Tawianese countryside.

South Korea

South Korea had imported Carabao mangoes from the neighbouring Philippines for years, but starting in 2008, the southern island of Jeju began growing high-value subtropical and tropical crops, including mangoes. This was made possible by a noticeable warming of the climate by 1.5°C (2.7 °F) in the last five years. To assist farmers in producing these new alternative crops, the government has established a new Agricultural Research Center for Climate Change.[14]

A small area in the south of the country, Gyeongnam, is also less affected by the cold continental high pressure in the winter and is able to produce quality mangoes. The Apple mango of Gyeongnam was chosen in 2021 as one of the 36 regional speciality crops for the 'national intensive nurturing of regional agriculture promotion project hosted by the Rural Development Administration'.[15] As a result of the new local availability, new culinary uses for mango are evolving in Korean cuisine. There are recipes for mango kimchi, and mango can be used as a substitute for Asian pear as a meat-tenderizing ingredient in Korean barbecue. The Apple mango, another name for the

Irwin mango, is named for its bright-red colour, round shape and sweet flavour. A clear, distilled spirit known as Apple mango soju is produced from these mangoes.

As in other Asian countries, mango is a popular flavour for desserts in South Korea. One particular dessert named 'Spring of the People', a mango mousse encased in a chocolate globe topped with edible flowers and a white chocolate map of Korea, managed to create an international diplomatic incident. In the spring of 2018, the South Korean delegation chose the dessert for a historic inter-Korean summit with Kim Jong-un. The map depicted on the dessert included a speck off the east coast of the peninsula representing the disputed Dokdo islands or Takeshima, claimed by both South Korea and Japan. The Japanese Ministry of Foreign Affairs formally lodged a complaint about the dessert, though apparently it was served anyway.

Making its way into Korean popular culture, K-pop singer Park Sun-young, known as Hyomin, uses mango in word-play in one of her 2018 hit songs, 'Mango', ordering her boyfriend to literally 'go away'– 'man go!' The visuals in the music video emphasize the luscious fruit, its vibrant colour and soft flesh. Korean K-pop group Super Junior has lasted an amazing seventeen years, longer than many of their fans have been alive, and has released a classic pop track called 'Mango'. The chorus emphasizes the sweetness of mangoes repeatedly. The accompanying music video features lots of mango colour and a mango fruit keychain.

Japan

The Japanese have a deeply held belief in a gift-giving tradition, *omiyage*, to show respect in business dealings, for special occasions, when returning from travelling or for honouring important social events like the arrival of an adored touring entertainer. In 2016, when Japanese fans of the pop star Lady Gaga were looking for the perfect gift for the mega-star who was touring in their country, they sent her a pair of beautiful mangoes. 'This mango is heaven!', she tweeted.

Mangoes were first introduced to Japan in the Meiji Period (1868–1912), though serious cultivation started in 1970. Only in 1985 was cultivation begun with the Irwin variety in Miyazaki Prefecture, where the climate is warm and there are long hours of sunlight.[16] Despite the fact that the climate in most of the country is not conducive to mango-growing, the Japanese hold the record for producing the world's most expensive mango, known as Taiyo no Tamago, 'Egg of the Sun', in Miyazaki Prefecture. Only about 15 per cent of the mangoes grown in the Miyazaki Prefecture on the southern island of Kyushu are classified as the highest grade. The vivid, deep-purple-red, perfectly formed and fibre-free mangoes must have a sugar content of 15 per cent or higher and weigh at least 950 grams (2 lbs). Mangoes that ripen and fall naturally from the tree have more

Miyazaki mango, known as 'Egg of the Sun'.

Mango Japanese sushi.

intense flavour and sweetness on the Brix scale. A labour-intensive technique of protective nets has been developed to allow the mangoes to fall naturally from the tree but not hit the ground. The temperature is carefully controlled in greenhouses at 20°C (68°F).[17]

The sum of ¥500,000 (U.S.$4,000) was the winning bid for a pair of these Miyazaki mangoes in spring 2022 at the annual auction in the Miyazaki Central Wholesale Market. This was more than double the price reached in the previous year's auction and matched a record high. The much-anticipated annual mango auction is held not so much to set a price for the mangoes as to honour the growers for their hard work. The buyers are often corporations or department stores who will use the luxury fruits for promotional displays.

Would the Japanese put mangoes on sushi? It would not be traditional, but now that sushi has become widely available in virtually every country worldwide, chefs are more inventive and experimental with toppings and components. Mango has visual and flavour appeal. Today there are even 'dessert sushi' recipes that use mango.

6

Sugary Sweet to Sharply Sour: Philippines, Southeast Asia, Australia and South Pacific

What do you serve a pope? Jessie Sincioco was the lucky chef chosen to craft Pope Francis's meals when he visited the Philippines in 2015. Shortly after the pope's departure, people started calling all three branches of Chef Jessie's restaurants, requesting to try whatever the Holy Father had eaten during his visit. The demand prompted Chef Jessie, nicknamed the Holy Chef, to create a menu of Pope Francis's favourite meals to serve in her restaurant, including her famous mango flambé for dessert. All of the profits from the sale of the special 'pope's meals' went to Tulay ng Kabataan, the orphanage near the main cathedral in Manila that the pontiff visited on his trip. Three years later, Chef Jessie visited the Vatican and presented the pope with a basket of sweet Philippine mangoes.

Mangoes are the national fruit of the Philippines, which has more than 7 million mango trees, grown mainly by smallhold farmers. Compared to other major crops grown in the Philippines, including rice, corn, coconut and sugarcane, mangoes are a high-value crop and are essential to the present-day national economy. The Carabao mango, also known as the Philippine mango, is particularly sweet and was named the sweetest mango in the *Guinness World Records* book in 1995.

Filipina food writer Doreen Gamboa Fernandez wrote in the essay 'Mangoes and Maytime', published in her book *Tikim: Essays on Philippine Food and Culture*,

> We wager that the mango memories of many a Filipino still revolve around the fruit ripening to fragrance in May-time . . . around mangoes peeled whole with the hands on farms and at feasts . . . to drip on chin and clothes; around mangoes chilled in river waters rather than in refrigerators, while feasters-to-be swim in the rivers of childhood; around mangoes sweet because stolen from consenting uncles or neighbors; around the fruit not as a commercial product but as a pledge of time and season and memory.[1]

Trade between the Spanish Asian territories, including the Philippines, the Spanish Viceroyalty of New Spain (Mexico) and other colonies of the New World was known as the Manila Galleon Trade.[2] Between 1565 and 1815, the Ataulfo and the Manolito mango cultivars that were brought to Mexico evolved from this trade and are sometimes called 'Manila mangoes'.[3]

The small island of Guimaras, located in the Western Visayas region in the Philippines, grows some of the world's sweetest mangoes. The capital, Jordan, is home to Our Lady of the Philippines Trappist Monastery, a Cistercian establishment founded in 1972. The Spanish brought Catholicism to the Philippines as well as Spanish culinary influences. The tradition of the Cistercian order is to provide their own food and living expenses through their own labour. The monks run a guest house, and making use of their local mangoes, they also produce jams and sweet foods, including mango *barquillos* (crispy

Manggahan Festival,
Guimaras, the Philippines.

biscuit rolls) and mango *biscocho* (bread baked with a layer of butter and sugar on top). Importing of mangoes or mango seeds onto the island of Guimaras is strictly prohibited by law as the location is a Special Quarantine Zone meant to protect the crop from pests and disease.

Filipinos love festivals, and the mango season is truly something to celebrate. The month-long Manggahan Festival on the island of Guimaras has been held annually each May since its inaugural event in 1993, and includes stunning mango-themed costumes for dance parades. Equally famous is the Dinamulag Mango Festival held at Zambales, and the two locations compete for the title of the sweetest mangoes. Cookbook writers Amy Besa and Romy Dorotan note in *Memories of Philippine Kitchens*, 'Naturally the Visayans will claim that Guimaras mangoes are the best, but in Luzon, Zambales mangoes are the

Dried green mangoes.

best because they are full of sweet, juicy pulp.'[4] A mango tart included in their book was featured on a *Martha Stewart Living* television programme in 1997.

Mango juice is also widely popular, and mango is a favourite flavour of locally made ice cream. Dried mangoes are eaten by the locals and are an important export product.

In contrast with the sweetness of Carabao and Zambales mangoes, Filipinos also love eating *manggang hilaw* (green, unripe mangoes) raw with rock salt, or with the fish paste *bagoong*. *Sinigang* is a sour-tasting soup often made with tangy tamarind, but green mangoes are used when in season to create this favourite comfort food, a Philippine version of chicken soup. Food writer Doreen Gamboa Fernandez was fond of a Philippine dish known as *kinilaw*, made with fresh fish with some similarities to ceviche. *Kinilaw* means 'eaten raw', and fresh green mango is often used as the souring agent.

A Philippine Department of Agriculture publication, *Philippine Mango Industry Roadmap* of 2018, summarizes some of the problems plaguing the mango industry in recent years. It has experienced competition from neighbouring countries such as Thailand and Australia which have entered the lucrative mango marketplace. In response, the *Roadmap* outlines goals that include investing in the rehabilitation of unproductive mango trees, improving post-harvest handling systems and adoption of the latest and best technology.[5]

Mangoes in Southeast Asia

Mangoes have been cultivated in Southeast Asia for thousands of years, likely spread by Buddhist pilgrims as early as the fourth century BCE. Geographic neighbours Vietnam, Thailand, Cambodia, Myanmar, Malaysia and Laos share a love of mangoes in their cuisines. While each country has developed its own unique dishes, many food preparations have similar ingredients and techniques, albeit with local names.

Following the lead of New York's moniker 'The Big Apple', in the 1990s the Thai Tourism Board coined the nickname 'The Big Mango' for Bangkok. In 2019 a group of Thai government agencies worked together to enter the *Guinness World Records* book for the largest serving of Thai mango sticky rice, presenting 5 tonnes of the dessert to 10,000 Chinese tourists. The event was part of the 'We Care About You' tourism initiative to entice more Chinese tourists.

Thai rapper Danupha 'MILLI' Khanatheerakul performed a song at the 2022 Coachella Valley Music and Arts Festival in California with lyrics praising mango sticky rice. During the performance, which quickly went viral, 'MILLI' ate a bowl of mango sticky rice on stage. The unusual idea evolved when a recording company asked the rapper to produce a track that represents Thailand. She chose to sing about her favourite dessert, explaining, 'Sticky rice also symbolizes the bond between me and my family because we always stick together.'[6]

The attention spurred enormous interest in Thai mango sticky rice and prompted the Thai Department of Cultural Promotion to begin the process of listing mango sticky rice as a UNESCO Intangible Cultural Heritage asset. It could be argued that it is through exposure to Thai cuisine that many Westerners are first introduced to mango in sweet desserts. Thai cuisine is known for its balance of four fundamental flavours in each dish, or in the overall meal: spicy, sour, sweet and salty. The ubiquitous Thai dessert *khao niaow ma muang*, mango with sticky rice and coconut sauce, appears on the menus of virtually every Thai restaurant.

The Thai government has a goal of making Thailand a major world food exporter, emphasizing quality standards and

Thai rapper MILLI at Coachella eating mango sticky rice, 2022.

technology under the ambitious slogan of 'Thailand: Kitchen of the World'. The popular mango sticky rice dessert has a major role to play. Thai restaurant chef Chutatip 'Nok' Suntaranon was a James Beard Foundation Award nominee in 2020 and her Philadelphia restaurant, Kalaya, was named Best New

Restaurant by *Esquire* magazine in 2021. Chef Nok keeps the classic dessert on her menu.

The Mango Art Festival was held in May 2022 in the River City area of Bangkok, with the hope of putting both Thai contemporary arts and Thai mangoes on the world stage. The event was promoted as 'Asia's first and only art festival that combines art, design and performance. Our goal is to develop Thailand's creative economy and demonstrate to the rest of the world what the country can do.'[7] Other mango festivals are held annually in Chiang Mai, where they crown a mango queen, and in Chachoengsao, a province just east of Bangkok. The Raed Paet, or Rhinoceros, mango grows in Chachoengsao, considered to be the best mango-growing region in the country. The name is a reference to the little pointed horn at the end of the fruit. Nam Dok Mai is a popular fibreless Thai mango variety introduced to Florida in 1973. The name means 'water of flower', or 'nectar'.

Mangoes are traditionally grown in the southern part of Vietnam, with the most prized coming from the Đồng Tháp region. Almost all of the mangoes produced in Vietnam are consumed within the country. There are many common uses of mangoes that differ from region to region, but green mango salad is a dish that every Vietnamese person eats and which can be found on the menu of almost any restaurant in Vietnam. Popularly known as *gỏi xoài*, the dish combines unripe mango with fish sauce or dried prawns. Other uses of green mango in Vietnam include unripe mangoes for making chutney and pickles. They are even eaten raw. The mango leaves are prepared as a vegetable similar to spinach and are used to flavour rice.

A similar popular dip served with green mango in Laos is known as *jeow mak muang*. Lao people jokingly say that a woman is pregnant if she craves sour green mangoes with a spicy sweet dipping sauce.[8] Laotians sun-dry mango purée as an efficient way of preserving the fruit.

In Cambodia, the unripe green mango is used as a sour spice in a Khmer sour soup called *samlo m'chu*, and the young mango leaves serve as a vegetable for *teuk kreung* and *prohok* (fish paste), everyday Khmer foods.[9] Typically using mango in pickles and side dishes, Cambodians also make mango salad using unripe or green mango mixed with shrimp, pork, chicken or dried fish. A favourite snack is green mango with salt, chilli or soy sauce. In 2021 Cambodia began exporting fresh mangoes directly to China as part of increased agricultural cooperation between the two countries.[10] The agreement for the shipment

Green mango pickles, Vietnam.

Mangoes in a market in Phnom Penh, Cambodia, 2019.

came after both countries paved the way by signing a protocol on phytosanitary requirements.

Perlis, the smallest state in Malaysia, is famous for the Harumani mango, the country's most prized and expensive mango. Malacca has its own variety named the Malacca Delite, unique because of its sweet, yellow-coloured flesh. Malacca

Delite mangoes can be used for juice. Entrepreneurs make pickles, *halwa* (fruit preserve in sugar syrup) and *rojak* (spicy fruit salad) from the mango. Kampung Gelam and its surrounding areas were once abandoned rice paddy fields, but now have been transformed into the state's main Malacca Delite cultivation area. More than 30,000 trees have been grown by some one hundred villagers since 2000, and there are plans to export the fruit and its by-products to the Middle East.[11]

Mangoes in Australia

In Australia, mangoes do not have the same deep religious and cultural connections found in South and Southeast Asia. A smaller native Australian version of the mango, *Buchanania obovate*, called the wild mango or green plum, is not in the genus *Mangifera*, but is from the same family, Anacardiaceae. This wild mango was a food source for the Aboriginal people of Australia and continues to be consumed today.[12] Experts on bush foods at the University of Queensland are working with the Aboriginal people in the Northern Territory to explore the commercial possibilities for this highly nutritious fruit.[13]

Botanical gardens established throughout the British colonies served a practical purpose much more important than providing weekend strolling grounds for the homesick colonists.[14] The economy of the colonial system was based on finding resources that could be supplied to the mother country, as well as providing new markets for their products. After the craze for exotic fruits based on all the New World edible discoveries of the 1700s, horticulturalists working worldwide in these newly created botanical gardens were charged with determining what new attractive cash crops could be grown in which new places.

Records show that Captain Curry of the British Royal Navy gifted a mango plant to Sydney's Botanic Gardens in 1823. As Commissioner of the Lands in Wide Bay in Queensland in the 1840s, J. C. Bidwell requested that some mango saplings be forwarded from the colonies in India, and he planted an orchard of the promising fruits. The survival of the saplings was only possible because of the recent development of the Wardian case, a box that kept the saplings alive on the long journey.[15]

In 1862, in the by-then booming colony of Queensland, the governor established the Queensland Acclimatisation Society specifically to import, test and introduce exotic plants for both economic and ornamental uses. The Kensington Pride mango, which now makes up 52 per cent of Australian mango production, was first grown in the late 1880s on an orchard named Kensington.[16]

Honey Gold mangoes were developed from the Kensington Pride mango, which was pollinated by an unknown mango variety in Queensland in 1991. Realizing it was a particularly successful hybrid, the plant breeders' rights were purchased by Piñata Farms, a family business that has greatly expanded the cultivation of this variety, which has a glossy yellow-orange skin and a spicy, distinct flavour. Piñata Farms is composed of thirty expert growers, and their marketing slogan asks the buyer to 'Trust us, we grew it,' using the latest techniques and technologies. One of these techniques is the practice of picking the mangoes at night, when the temperature is cooler, which is better for both the workers and the mangoes. New machinery was developed that illuminates the mangoes on the trees, making them easier to spot by the pickers, but the growers had to find ways to combat the bats and bugs that were attracted to the light at night.[17]

On iconic Bondi Beach in Sydney, there is a popular annual mango festival that officially welcomes summer in Australia and includes mango-eating competitions and the sale of mango products. The event, called the Mess-tival, celebrates the messy tactile pleasure of eating a juicy mango.

Mangoes in the South Pacific

Brought from the Philippines as part of the Manila Galleon, Captain John Meek delivered a batch of mango plants to Hawaii. The plants were divided between Don Francisco de Paula Marín, a Spanish horticulturist with an estate in Honolulu, and a missionary based in Maui. Don Marín arrived in Hawaii in 1793 at the age of twenty and became a permanent resident of the islands. He accumulated extensive property on which he introduced the cultivation of many fruits, including grapes, oranges and pineapples, as well as mangoes. Speaking multiple languages, including Hawaiian, he became a trusted adviser to King Kamehameha, who granted him multiple plots of land. Don Marín's nickname, Manini, means 'stingy' in the Indigenous Hawaiian dialect, which reportedly was appropriate since he was known to be unwilling to share the seeds of the plants he imported.

In 1899 S. W. Damon introduced into Hawaii several grafted trees from Indian varieties. In 1903 the Hawaii Agricultural Experiment Station was established for the purpose of agricultural research to assist in commercial development of agricultural products. Part of their research involved testing multitudes of mango varieties for adaptability and quality.[18]

A popular mango product in Hawaii is *li hing* mango, sold either wet or dry in what are known as 'crack-seed stores'. A snack that made its way to Hawaii with Chinese immigrants from Zhongshan, China, *li hing mui* translates as 'travelling plum'. The term 'crack-seed' is now used to refer to all types of

Edible mango products, Hawaii.

preserved fruits, but it is also a reference to a type of preserved plum treated with salt and spices. The plum pit is literally cracked open and marinated in sweet flavouring.[19] Popular Hawaiian mango pickles are often made using *li hing mui*, giving it a distinct flavour and pink colour. The vendor of a variety of marijuana seeds called Mr Mango Crack makes some very enticing claims: 'The terpenic cocktail that will serve this weed to your taste buds is first class, a masterful combination of earthy, sweet, citrus, sweet mango and very pungent Skunk notes. Invigorating and energetic, it brings you to a state of happiness and good vibes that need to be shared.'[20]

Primarily a tourist destination and tourist economy, Hawaii may win the award for the most mango festivals, from Mangoes at the Moana to Mango Jam Honolulu and numerous other celebrations spread throughout the islands. Many varieties of mangoes grow throughout Hawaii and the South Pacific, ripening at different times, ensuring year-round availability.

Statue of the Hindu diety Ganesha with *barfi*.

7

Mangoes, Metaphors and Meanings

The characteristics of the mango have made the fruit a popular metaphor in parts of the world where it grows. The vivid colourations, intense smell, sweet taste and sensuous, drippy texture speak of desirability in the arts, song, literature and poetry. The seasonality of the blossoms and fruiting references abundance when mango is available and desire and anticipation when it is not. The mango is frequently used as a metaphor in the religions of South Asia. Both the fruit and the tree feature prominently in stories that teach the principles of Hinduism, Buddhism and Jainism.

Mangoes and Hinduism, Buddhism and Jainism

A famous Hindu legend describes this quandary over a desirable golden mango. The visitor, a sage named Narada, arrives with only one gift, a golden mango, but there are two children. What parent hasn't been faced with that problem? The parents, the Hindu deities Shiva and his lovely wife, the goddess Parvati, decide to have a competition between their two sons,

Ganesha and Kartikeya, to decide which child will win the prized mango.

The challenge is to determine which brother can circle the world three times the fastest. The chubby elephant-headed brother, Ganesha, uses his wits and a large dose of flattery to prevail. While Kartikeya, the handsome and athletic brother, rushes off to completely circle the world physically, Ganesha merely walks in a circle around his parents, explaining simply that his loving parents are his whole world. Ganesha wins the golden mango. Beyond the most obvious meaning of the story – that it pays to curry favour with one's parents – another, more complex meaning would be that some people gather knowledge by travelling the wide world, while others stay in one place carefully observing their immediate world. The mango in Hinduism compares with the apple in the Christian faith as a knowledge-giving object of desire.

Ganesha, the remover of obstacles, a popular Hindu deity who helps one succeed in new journeys and challenges, is often represented dancing under a fruiting mango tree. Mangoes represent prosperity and good luck in the Hindu tradition. In Hindu weddings throughout India, Ganesha is invoked before the marriage rituals begin to ensure that the ceremony goes smoothly and the marriage is successful. It is not surprising that mango dishes are often part of wedding feasts. *Aamras*, made of mango purée and cardamom, is traditionally served, as well as *mango dal* and raw *mango panha*.

Because the deities Shiva and Parvati are believed to have been married under a mango tree, mango leaves are often used to decorate marriage venues. The image of a mango tree entwined with creepers or vines is a symbolic metaphor referring to the relationship of the partners in a good marriage.

The *Mongo Mango Cookbook* describes some elaborate rituals and local customs related to marriage ceremonies in parts

Aamras, a traditional Indian wedding dish.

of India.[1] For example, at a Bengali wedding, a copper pot filled with mango leaves is placed under a pair of small banana trees on each side of the entrance to the ceremony. A traditional South Indian gold bridal necklace, called a *mango mala*, is adorned with mango-shaped stones, representing the wish for a fertile marriage and to have many children.

An old tradition once practised in some parts of India was to have the groom 'marry' a mango tree, performing the same rites he would have done during the marriage ceremony.

Hindu bridal necklace, *mango mala*.

A 'mango wedding', or *ul bapla* or *amba biha*, might be performed before the actual human wedding.[2] The ritual was thought to confer fertility on the couple and pay homage to the power of nature to sustain human life. Simply having a mango tree on one's property is considered auspicious when terms of an arranged marriage are being determined. In Bengali folk tradition, the bridegroom must chew tender mango leaves before the marriage ritual, with the mango symbolizing masculinity in this case.

Providing a wedding dowry for a female child in India may be a heavy burden on a family and lead to female infanticide. In some villages in the northern state of Bihar, parents are directed to plant ten mango saplings when a female child is born to ease this burden. The money from the sale of the fruits of these trees contributes to the girl's dowry and wedding expenses. The tree is considered to be a guardian for the child, according to film director Kunal Sharma, who made a documentary called *Mango Girls*.[3] A villager from Dharhara in her film notes, 'We treat a girl child as the incarnation of goddess Lakshmi, the Hindu Goddess of wealth.'[4]

Ganesha loves sweets and is known as Modakpriya, meaning 'the one who loves *modak*', a dumpling-shaped sweet consumed in large quantities during the ten days of his festival, Ganesha Chaturthi. A *puja*, or special prayer ritual, for Ganesha can conclude with an offering of 101 *modaks* being presented to Ganesha as *prasadam*, or specially blessed food, which is then distributed to participants. *Modak* can be flavoured with mango, as can many other popular sweets such *laddoos*, ball-shaped sweets, or *barfi*, similar to a rich fudge.

Thousands of mangoes are offered to Ganesha during the Akshaya Tritiya, an annual festival that falls in the mango season. After first being offered to the deity, the golden fruit is then distributed to devotees. The celebration is considered an auspicious time for beginning new ventures, marriages or days of remembrance for those who have passed away.

The two most important stories in the Hindu faith are the *Ramayana* and the *Mahabharata*, both of which contain numerous references to the mango fruit and the mango tree. According to some stories, Hanuman, the brave monkey warrior in the *Ramayana*, brought the mango tree from Lanka (Sri Lanka) to India. The god Vishnu, the preserver, reappears in many forms or avatars, and on one occasion he appears as a dwarf mango tree in the Dandaka forest, where the hero Rama and his wife Sita are exiled. The mango tree form of Vishnu is his only plant avatar, and appearing in this form emphasizes the belief that plants are important parts of the universe.

The mango is the national fruit of India and the national tree of Bangladesh. Trees are a fundamental element in the Hindu religion and considered sacred. In ancient holy books, the mango tree is characterized as *Kalpavriksha* or 'wish-granting'. Planting a mango tree is considered a spiritual act that includes the responsibility to properly care for the tree or mango grove as one would as a parent of a daughter. This includes even the task of finding an appropriate mate for the tree itself. A tamarind tree is usually the preferred groom for the mango tree during this symbolic rite, which must be undertaken before adults can eat the fruit of the tree. In Nepal, one tradition intended to ensure a good harvest is the practice of ritually marrying a mango tree with a well as a source of water in the orchard.[5]

In South Asia, mango tree leaves are considered auspicious and associated with prosperity and happiness. Five, seven or eleven fresh mango leaves, symbolizing life and fertility, are an integral part of the arrangement of the Hindu Kalasha, a water pot used in the *puja* prayer rituals. The vessel contains water and a coconut resting on mango leaves, symbolizing the goddess Lakshmi, and is believed to keep out negative energy.[6] Mango leaves are used during almost all Hindu ceremonies, often strung as garlands, or *thoran*, for festivals and weddings.[7]

The festival of Ugadi, or Yugadi, marks the beginning of the new year for Hindus in the states of Karnataka, Andhra Pradesh and Telangana in India. The traditional drink *Ugadi Pachadi* is much anticipated. First offered to the deities, the beverage brings together all six flavours (*shadruchulu*) that the palate desires, acknowledging that one must accept all the various experiences in life: sweet jaggery and banana pieces represent happiness; tamarind symbolizes sourness or unpleasantness;

salty symbolizes fear; neem flower represents bitterness or sadness; and spicy green chilli represents anger. The sixth ingredient in the recipe, unripe mango, symbolizes the element of surprise in one's life.[8]

Mangoes and Buddhism

There are countless examples of the importance of mango and the mango tree in the teachings of Buddhism. As the image of the Buddha evolved, one of the characteristics noted is that he had a rounded chin shaped like a mango stone.[9] In Thailand, there are many examples of the Buddha figure holding a mango in his hand, one of the official positions in Thai Buddhism.

Buddhists are urged to follow the Middle Path and not extremes, but the most important guiding principle is *ahimsa*, or non-violence. Prohibited from consciously doing harm to animals themselves, monks are able to eat meat or fish when it is offered to them as alms, but a diet of plants is preferable. Fasting is practised as a way of controlling earthly desires. A Buddhist would be expected to abstain from food from noon until dawn the next day. Eating a mango is forbidden during the period of abstention from food, but mango juice could be imbibed all day. Carrying this sweet fruit along on their journey to teach Buddha's message, Buddhist monks also spread the seeds of the mango throughout Southeast Asia and China.

Early Buddhist images include female tree spirits called *yakshi*, who were so fertile that their mere touch caused a tree to blossom or fruit. *Yakshis* gracefully swaying beneath mango trees are depicted kicking the tree trunks and touching the branches, which are laden with fruit. Examples are carved on the earliest Buddhist monuments, including on the famous Buddhist stupa Sanchi, which contains the relics of the Buddha

Seated Buddha holding mango, Thailand, 18th–19th century, gilt bronze.

Yakshi under mango tree, Great Stupa at Sanchi, 1st century BCE– 1st century CE.

himself. A monkey is depicted offering a bowl of honey to a mango tree representing the Buddha in a carving on the stupa.[10]

Important events in the life of the historical Buddha are connected to the mango tree. Buddha preaches his first sermon under a mango tree. Amrapali, the wealthy courtesan who converted to Buddhism, gifted her entire mango orchard to Buddha, providing him with a comfortable place to rest. The Buddha's first stop on his journey to enlightenment was Vaisali, where lush mango trees lined the path. Even Buddha's passing on to Nirvana is said to have taken place after his last meal, which had been offered while he visited the mango grove of Cunda Kammaraputta.

One of the most famous miracles that Buddha performed is known as the 'Twin Miracle', during which Buddha emitted fire from the top half of his body and water from the bottom. The demonstration followed a challenge by rival religious leaders. Buddha declared he would perform this miracle beneath a mango tree, though his rivals had schemed to destroy all the fruit trees to prevent the miracle Buddha planned. Buddha then caused a full-grown mango tree to appear from a single mango gifted to him by a humble gardener.[11] The re-enacting of this feat has evolved into a popular magic act performed by Indian street magicians still today.

Indian mango tree trick, *c.* 1870, photograph by Willoughby Wallace Hooper.

Buddhism uses stories to teach the principles of the faith, and many of these stories include mangoes. These stories of Buddha's former lives are known as the *Jatakas*, in which he appears in many forms, animal and human, practising non-violence. One of the most famous *Jatakas* is the *Monkey Jataka*, involving particularly juicy mangoes on a tree near a riverbank. A tribe of monkeys enjoy the fruit. The tree is discovered by a covetous king who sends his armed soldiers to gather all the fruit for himself. The monkey king sacrifices himself by creating a bridge to allow his tribe to escape, illustrating the importance of putting the lives of others before one's self.[12]

In another story illustrating the medicinal use of mango, Bimbadevi eschews the wealth and privileges of her nobility to become a follower of Buddha. One day she becomes ill with stomach pains caused by flatulence. She had formerly cured her recurrent ailment with mango juice and sugar but, as a poor ascetic, she no longer had access to those items. A disciple of Buddha informs the king of Bimbadevi's illness. The king sends her sweetened mango juice and she is cured. After that, the king sends her sugared mango juice every day.[13]

The *Amba Jataka* is a story involving an evil ascetic who keeps all the mangoes in a grove for himself. This selfish conduct is observed by a bodhisattva, an enlightened being who is on the path to Buddhahood, who vows to teach the ascetic a lesson by destroying all the mangoes. A ferocious monster frightens the guilty ascetic away after he wrongly accuses others of the destruction.

Jainism, founded in India about the same time as Buddhism (around 500 BCE), is a religion that emphasizes extreme non-violence. The Jain goddess Ambika is worshipped as a patron of mothers and infants, traditionally represented sitting under a mango tree on a lion and holding a mango in her right hand. The description of an example in the collection of the Victoria

Monkeys in mango tree, detail from an Indian painting, *c.* 1810, tempera, ink and gold on paper.

and Albert Museum notes that the mango is associated with 'rounded female forms, especially breasts . . . underscored by the similarity between the words for mango in Sanskrit (*amra*) and Hindi (*amb*, *amba*) and likewise the words for mother (*amba* and *amma*, respectively)'.[14]

Mango in Literature

In addition to many references in religious oral traditions and written literature, the mango is a potent metaphor in prose and poetry. It is associated with fertility and is considered to be an aphrodisiac. The name of the Hindu God of Love, Kamadeva, derives from the two terms *kama*, sensuous love, and *deva*, heavenly or divine. The arrows of Kamadeva's bow are tipped with the essence of sweet-smelling flowers, including mango blossoms. Kamadeva is related to the god Vishnu, who takes on multiple forms. Kamadeva is often depicted as a handsome young man seated on a parrot. The bird symbolizes a messenger and a storyteller, his red beak representing love's passion and his green body representing fertility.[15]

The mango is sometimes called 'the love fruit' and is the only fruit for which there is a position named in the famous Indian love manual, the *Kama Sutra*: *amrachushita* means 'sucking a mango'. The process of budding and fruiting serves as a metaphor for the spring and summer seasons. 'As the mango flowers begin to swell, to put forth sprouts, to bud and finally to blossom, love too swelled, sprouted, budded and blossomed.'[16]

Mahatma Gandhi enjoyed luscious mangoes for much of his life. There are numerous occasions in which Gandhi used the mango and mango tree as a metaphor to teach his messages.

> Plant a mango sapling and see what happens if you fail to water it for two or three days or to make a hedge around it . . . The mango tree, as it grows and spreads, bends lower. Similarly, as the strength of the strong increases, he should become progressively more humble, he should become more and more god-fearing.[17]

Here's another example from Gandhi: 'Mango trees do not bear fruit quickly. If a tree like the mango tree requires to be tended for a number of years, how much tender care will a woman require who is like a tree and who has been kept ignorant for so long?'[18] In his later years, however, after indulging in a gift of some mangoes sent as 'medicine', Gandhi said, 'Mango is a cursed fruit. We must get used to not treating it with so much affection.' He believed his attraction to sensual mangoes was an attachment to the material world of senses that he struggled to transcend.[19]

Mango can also symbolize sensuality in American popular culture. A well-known episode of the sitcom *Seinfeld* that aired in 1993, called 'The Mango', featured the characters Kramer and George discovering the aphrodisiac qualities of the fruit, which assisted their love lives.

Mangoes are associated with female body parts, including the perfect female breast shape, and a shapely rear end. In E. M. Forster's novel *A Passage to India*, Dr Aziz promises Dr Fielding, 'I shall arrange a lady with breasts like mangoes.' Author Salman Rushie describes a memorable scene in *Midnight's Children* in which the narrator inadvertently sees his own mother's naked rear end, referring to it as the 'Black Mango'.

The mango tree, sometimes called the 'lover of the cuckoo', is associated with the cuckoo bird, which is often illustrated and poetically described by Rajashekhara in his guide for poets, the *Kāvyamīmāṃsā*, as perched on a mango branch in springtime. The bird becomes intoxicated and his voice becomes passionate while sucking in the fragrant nectar of the mango blossoms.[20]

Mango is the only fruit that has its own literary genre, 'sari-mango' literature, a term coined by several male South Asian writers in 2013. The term is intended as a criticism of fiction written by mostly female South Indian writers for referencing saris and mangoes as cliché and catering to their Western readers' expectations for 'otherness' and exotica. Award-winning South Asian author Salman Rushdie stated, 'I have a rule that I offer to young writers. There must be no tropical fruits in the title. No mangoes. No guavas. None of those. Tropical animals are also problematic. Peacock, etc. Avoid that shit.'[21] It is noteworthy that Rushdie himself mentions mangoes more than twenty times, including in references to a character's breast in his prize-winning novel *Midnight's Children*.

Often emphasizing childhood memories and culinary nostalgia, there are many novels with 'mango' in the title, written by authors from virtually all countries where mangoes are grown, from the Caribbean to the Philippines and the South Pacific. Indian writer Amulya Malladi, author of *The Mango Season*, writes of the main character's visit from the United States to her home in India at a time when the family traditionally made mango pickles. She intends to marry her African American

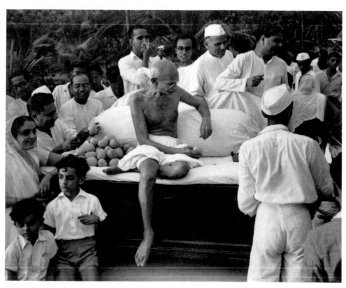

Mahatma Gandhi distributing mangoes to children, 1944.

fiancé but is warned, 'You cannot make mango pickle with tomatoes . . . You cannot mesh two cultures without making a mess of it.'[22] 'Two women, two cultures, and the fight to find a new life in America' summarizes the theme of the novel *Mango Bride* by Philippine writer Marivi Soliven. Soliven describes a nostalgic scene in which 'The familiar sweet fragrance lifted Beverly back to long-gone childhood Sundays . . . Beverly picked up a mango and breathed in the scent of home.'[23] Cuban-American writer Berta Isabel Arias relates a children's story about a place where one can drink from sweet mango rivers in her novel *Mango Rain*.

The present popularity of culinary memoirs and cookbooks includes many books featuring mangoes by authors from the Philippines to the Caribbean. Examples include Indian chef Madhur Jaffrey's *Climbing the Mango Trees*, *Mango and Peppercorns* by Tung Nguyen, Katherine Manning and Lyn Nguyen, and *Mangoes and Curry Leaves* by Jeffrey Alford and Naomi Duguid.

An astonishing number of children's books currently in print, authored by writers from the whole mango diaspora, reference mangoes in their titles. The growing diversity in the U.S. population, which includes immigrants from many mango-growing countries, suggests the fruit can function as a 'gateway' food that can introduce a culture and cuisine. Writers have fond memories of their childhood activities that involved eating the messy fruit. The topic lends itself to lessons of sharing, as a single tree produces hundreds of fruits. *A Season for Mangoes*, by Jamaican author Regina Hansom, relates the story of the main character's first 'sit up', a traditional memorial celebration in Jamaica, involving her grandmother's favourite mangoes. Hidayah Amin, a Malay Singaporean writer, tells the story of a mango planted at the time of her birth that she follows through her lifetime in *The Mango Tree*. Indian diaspora writer Malavika

Shetty gives charming details of friendships and mango treats in her book, *The Sweetest Mango*.

There is a long history of poets making use of the mango fruit and mango trees as metaphors in South Asian love poetry. It was a surprise and a bit of a mystery to her fans when American pop singer Ariana Grande shared this poem by thirteenth-century Indo-Persian Sufi poet and musician Amir Khusrau in a tweet in 2019:

> He visits my town once a year.
> He fills my mouth with kisses and nectar
> I spend all my money on him.
> *Who girl, your man?*
> No, a mango.[24]

Kalidasa was a well-known Sanskrit poet and playwright from the thirteenth century, who used mango blossoms to represent love in the springtime. A unique festival, known as Aam aur Ghalib, is held each summer in India in honour of the celebrated eighteenth-century Urdu Indian poet Mirza Ghalib, who was a genuine mango aficionado. Poems are read and buckets of mangoes are devoured. The poet is known for his assertion that the best mangoes should be sweet and plentiful. The Indian poet and 1913 Nobel Prize-winner Rabindranath Tagore sets the scene for his poem 'Unyielding' with the first lines: 'When I called you in your garden/ Mango blooms were rich in fragrance.'[25]

John Agard, an Afro-Guyanese playwright, poet and children's writer, composed a love poem about a young English woman's first taste of mangoes, but the poem has deeper meanings about cultural differences, and it critiques colonialization. Sarcastic and bitter, these lines relating a conversation begin 'Self Portrait as Mango', a poem by American poet Tarfia Faizullah, who was born to Bangladeshi immigrants and uses the image of the mango as a sharp tool for criticism of perceived discrimination: 'She says, *Your English is great. How long have you been in our country?*/ I say, *Suck on a mango, bitch, since that's all you think I eat anyway.*'[26]

The mango and mango tree are useful metaphorical images used in a unique traditional Indian art form that combines poetry, music and painting. Ragas are musical modes or forms creating specific moods, which are accompanied by verses dealing with both happiness and pain in love. Ragas are often illustrated by detailed miniature paintings called *ragamalas*. Each of the six main ragas has an appropriate *ragin*, female image, and the paintings must include visual clues that tell the story. Mango trees in flower tell the viewer it is springtime, in a popular example known as the *Vasant Ragini*. Trees full of ripened mangoes indicate summer, as in the *Kakubha Ragini*, which depicted both tenderness and sadness, as the heroine is separated from her lover.[27]

If the flowering and fruiting of the mango tree are used to set the location, timing and mood for musical modes in Indian *ragamalas*, the same might be said of mangoes featured in the lyrics of anonymous folk songs of the Caribbean; Jamaican songs 'Mango Walk' and 'Mango Time' reflect the sense of celebration and enjoyment of the mango harvest.

There are examples of contemporary music groups worldwide from Japan to Jamaica who rap and rock with mango references in their songs and lyrics. Mango Grove is a South African Afropop band whose music combines the music of townships with international pop. Mango Records is a record label founded in 1972 that focuses on Caribbean music.

A genre of music in the Caribbean known as 'chutney music' combines the sounds of African and Indian influences. Who wouldn't be seduced by the crooning of Ursula Andress as she emerges from the ocean in the 1962 James Bond film *Dr. No*, singing about finding herself and her lover underneath a mango tree about to make *boolooloup* soon.[28] Jimmy Buffett's 'Last Mango in Paris' vividly defines an escapist island lifestyle.

Mangoes in the Visual Arts

Botanical illustrators documenting the flora and fauna of South Asia painted detailed renderings of mangoes in the sixteenth century. However, in 1887 Post-Impressionist painter Paul Gauguin recognized the artistic potential of this fruit while he worked on the Caribbean island of Martinique, painting *Two Tahitian Women*. Later, travelling to Tahiti, Gauguin featured mangoes as the equivalent of the apple in the Garden of Eden in many of his paintings. The artist eroticized both the fruit and the tropical setting. In a movie review of the 2018 biopic *Gauguin: Voyage to Tahiti*, it is noted, 'He (Gauguin) wants her (his young Tahitian lover) bare-breasted and chewing on a mango.'[29] Another reviewer writes, 'There are a few tactile moments: Gauguin slowly eating a mango.'[30] In Gauguin's painting *Tahitian Eve*, the mango blossoms on the platter held by innocent female figures suggests the sexuality of the fruitful breasts bursting from those blossoms.

An interesting story about cows in India eating mango leaves may account for the vivid, yellow colours in the paintings of another Post-Impressionist painter, Vincent Van Gogh, and of the British landscape painter Joseph Turner. Although some art historians doubt the veracity of the story, in an 1883 letter to the Society of Arts in London, T. N. Mukharji, reporting from Bihar province in India, recounted how Indian yellow pigment was made. This bright-orange-yellow pigment originated in the fifteenth century under the Mughals and became

Paul Gauguin, *Two Tahitian Women*, 1899, oil on canvas.

known to European artists shortly thereafter. Mukharji reported that farmers were able to force cows to urinate into buckets on command after being allowed to roam in a mango orchard where they ate mango leaves. The urine was then collected, concentrated, filtered and made into balls set out in the sun to dry, eventually resulting in the pigment. The downside to this process is that mango leaves can be toxic to livestock if eaten in large quantities. This process of manufacturing Indian yellow pigment was later deemed to constitute cruelty to animals and was outlawed.[31]

'Mango' is also a colour, but not so easily defined. The Pantone company, which provides a standardized colour-matching system, lists sample 14–1140 TSX as 'Iced Mango', while Pantone 15–0960 TPG is 'Mango Mojito'. Various paint brands offer 'Mango Margarita', 'Mango Punch', 'Ripe Mango' and 'Mango Madness'. Art supplies company Crayola has a crayon named Mango Tango; another, Mango, is a much lighter yellow.

Contemporary Caribbean painters, including Willy Jean-Paul, a Haitian artist working in Key West, Florida, create colourful market scenes with vibrant baskets of mangoes. Haitian artist Celestin Faustin (1948–1981) envisioned a Caribbean Garden of Eden with Adam and Eve luxuriating beneath a fruit-laden mango tree. Mexican artist Frida Kahlo (1907–1954) included mangoes in her colourful still-life paintings. Possibly the most unusual example of mango painting would be *Under the Mango Tree*, one of the very few paintings by author D. H. Lawrence, which is also an erotic reference to the Adam and Eve story. Most authorities at the time considered his paintings too erotic to be exhibited in Great Britain. Lawrence makes numerous references to mangoes in his writing, particularly in his *Mornings in Mexico*, in which his short stories emphasize the exoticism of the Mexican landscape to the Western reader.

Widely regarded in South Asia as an auspicious symbol, the stylized image of the mango in the form of the paisley motif is ubiquitous, from bandanas to wallpaper, to the famous shawls, clearly echoing its shape. While there are several explanations for the derivation of the motif, the paisley design is called *ambi* in Punjabi, the root *amb* meaning 'mango'. Paisley is the name of the town in Scotland to which the beautiful patterned shawls, originally laboriously handwoven, were imported from South

Asia by the East India Company. The beautiful shawls with their distinctive mango-shaped motifs became a symbol of wealth and status and were soon produced by machine in the industrial textile mills in Paisley, Scotland.[32] As a reflection of the wider availability of the fruit in Europe and the United States and the usefulness of the image in metaphorical communication, a mango emoji was approved as part of Unicode in 2018.[33]

8

Mango Miracle: Future of Mangoes

Can mangoes become the next 'avocado toast'? Will Americans and Europeans ever have access to truly wonderful fresh mango varieties that appeal to all five senses? Can researchers and producers find the sweet spot between a practical product that ships and stores well for the commercial market but also retains its deliciousness? There are multiple challenges and opportunities for mangoes and mango-growers in the years to come.

The National Mango Board's mission is to increase the consumption of mangoes in the United States and Europe, working with international growers and producers. They hope to tap into the potential in these markets by educating consumers about the flavour and nutrition of mangoes, as well as the history and culture of the fruit, while bringing the international industry together. The board's vision is for mangoes to transition from an exotic fruit treat to an accessible, ubiquitous and popular food product in the Western world, as it is in countries where it grows. A national mango retailer of the year is selected that the board notes has identified mango as an 'opportunity item' for potentially increased sales. As the demographics of the United States change, increasingly larger communities from Asian and Hispanic countries will demand better-quality mangoes and more extensive varieties, recalling the fruit of their home countries.

More than ever, consumers are interested in globally inspired foods. The fact that mangoes are largely not grown in the United States or Europe allows the fruit to retain an element of the exotic. Mango is a familiar ingredient in South Asian, African, South American and Central American cuisines and inspires fusion restaurant chefs worldwide. Market research has shown that adding mangoes to the description of dishes on a restaurant menu enhances the chances of their selection.[1]

Consumers continue to look for what the food industry calls 'plant-centric' options, choosing less red meat for environmental and health reasons. Obviously, mango slaw is healthier than a cheeseburger![2] Studies, such as those recently completed at the University of Palermo, Sicily, investigate the phytonutrient properties of mangoes and their potential health benefits.

Mangoes for sale featuring educational marketing labels.

Sardines and mango, Catalina Oliver Ors restaurant, Palma de Mallorca, Spain.

Inspired by the success of trendy avocado toast, mango marketers are developing products targeting breakfast: mango juice combinations, kefir, yoghurt smoothies and even mango oatmeal and congee as a healthy way to start the day.

In South Asia, babies have traditionally enjoyed mango pits as delicious and satisfying teethers and pacifiers for centuries. Only since 2007 have babies in the Western world been introduced to the joys of mango in baby food products made by the largest baby food manufacturing company in the United States, the Gerber company. Mango producers hope that the now-more-familiar taste and bright colour will produce a new generation of mango-lovers. Healthy dried mango fruit snacks, mango 'leather' and gummies even appear on grocery shelves worldwide. Creative new snack foods such as mango- and

Innovative protective mango packaging.

chilli-lime-flavoured potato chips, mango and sticky rice spring rolls, and mango-coconut-flavoured caramel corn appear on shelves. Manufacturers are testing the market with freeze-dried mango chips and on-the-go healthy alternative fruit snack pouches of mango purée for busy adults and children's lunches.

Ready-made mango salsas and barbecue sauces abound. Mango-flavoured vinaigrettes are available to top fresh salads that feature chopped dried mango. From France to Japan, customers can purchase everything from mango macarons to mango mochi. Mango-flavoured salt even appears on market shelves in Spain.

Research programmes in many countries and universities are aimed at helping the entire mango supply chain deliver a quality product and also educate growers, shippers, packers, importers and retailers. Importers are experimenting with different types of packaging that can deliver the perfectly uniform fruit that U.S. consumers have learned to expect. Noris Ledesma received a patent in 2022 for the mango variety she developed named Cherry, which has a brilliant red-purple peel, camouflaging imperfections so noticeable on the available Ataulfo mangoes. Retailers are also attempting to assure the buyer that, the same as with those misshapen heirloom tomato varieties, a perfectly delicious mango can include an occasional brown spot and unusual shape. Producers and distributors have learned that a mango variety like Ataulfo, named after a Mexican farmer, rechristened as Honey or Champagne will be more appealing to American consumers.[3]

Similar to the goals of the heirloom tomato movement, researchers and growers, particularly in India, are working to protect many of the delicious and unique traditional mango varieties that could disappear in the rush to make the distribution of mangoes more practical. We hope the future sees the wide availability of fresh mangoes beyond a 'standard supermarket

Noris Ledesma holding her Cherry mango variety.

mango' and offers more examples of the extensive variety of colour, shape, size, smell, texture and even messy, sucking sound that makes mangoes so very special.

Experimental programmes are developing products that can be made from the 'waste' – that is, the skin and pit – resulting from processing mangoes for their pulp and juice. Mango peel makes up 15–20 per cent of the total weight of the fruit. The peel can be dried and made into a powder that is added to energy bars to increase the fibre content. The kernel inside the pit can be pressed to make an oil that can be used in chocolate processing. Fruitleather Rotterdam is a company that produces vegan leather from mango waste that is generated by

Mango products, freeze-dried and puréed.

Mango drinks for all occasions, from relaxing teas to energy drinks.

the quality testing required for importing mangoes to Europe. There is ongoing research in India on how to make this process more efficient and profitable. ABC Fruits, one of the leading fruit pulp manufacturers in India, uses waste mango fibre in dietary supplements, and mango peel to create herbal extracts.[4]

Noting a sunnier side of climate change, farmers are finding it is now possible to successfully grow mangoes in surprising new areas such as Sicily and South Korea. Additional mango-growing micro-climates are likely to emerge, making mangoes a local fruit option for more consumers globally. Wong Farms has developed the technology to grow mangoes in the sandy soil, desert heat and humidity of Mecca, California, by inserting microchips into the trees that monitor the water pressure in the plant to determine an efficient drip irrigation schedule. In a less technological solution to the damage from too much sun, their mangoes are protected in brown- and white-paper lunch bags, which are later recycled back into the soil.[5]

Many countries in the Caribbean and Africa, where mangoes have long been a part of the local cuisine, have only begun to export mangoes in recent years because of technological advances, improvements in transport and better disease and pest control. Initiatives such as the Haiti Hope Project: Message in a Mango, a public–private partnership between TechnoServe, Coca-Cola and a coalition of business and international government agencies, aims to help small-hold farmers in developing countries with an emphasis on the role of women.[6]

In Kenya, 40–45 per cent of the annual mango crop is often lost because of pests, disease or poor handling techniques. In order to help address this, a project under the organization UN Women aided by Jomo Kenyatta University of Agriculture and Technology, Stockholm Environment Institute and the Rockefeller Foundation was created to provide training and processing machinery to be shared by small-farm coalitions.[7]

The Cambodian Mango Processing Facility Project sponsored by Angkor Harvest, a private-sector mango export company, has the goal of providing 'a consistent outlet for the sale of mangoes and a platform on which to build a national brand'. One of their efforts is to directly link Cambodian mango farmers to export markets, increasing profits for the farmers.[8]

Some of the technological advances under development intended to improve the efficiency and profitability of mango cultivation for the future are bound to conflict with the romanticized memories described nostalgically in diaspora fiction and culinary memoirs. For example, if Ultra-High Density Plantation (UHDP) methods are adopted, there would no longer be the need to climb up into mango trees, which would be pruned into slim hedges or espaliered on supports.[9] Mango Off-Season Technology (MOST) involves the application of a growth regulator, a form of hormone that has the ability to adjust the yearly traditional timing of the flowering and fruiting of crops. Veny Marti, owner of Martex Farms in Santa Isabel, Puerto Rico, notes that using growth regulators can be especially useful in climates where there is no seasonal variation in temperature. Mango farmers would be able to decide the optimal time to harvest their crop for the highest profit, but the concept of the anticipation of a shared season of mango abundance would be lost.[10]

We already expect to find mango as a flavour choice for smoothies at our local cafés and dried mangoes as a snack choice. We hope that in the future we can also share the passionate sensual experience of consuming the best fresh mangoes and the pleasure of indulging in mangoes in new forms. The future looks very bright for all forms of this sunny, stimulating versatile fruit.

Recipes

Mango Dinner Menu

We invite you to create your own memorable mango-themed event with suggestions below for each course. Perhaps plan a celebration of World Mango Day on 22 July. Or, try to imitate the feast thrown by the fourteenth-century Mughal emperor Alauddin Khalji, in which every dish incorporated mango in some way.

Cocktails and Drinks

Mango lassi
Mango wine
Tropical mango cocktail
Mango leaf tea
Ugadi Pachadi (India)

Starters

Aamras (mango wedding soup) (India)
Raw mango *rasam*, soup (India)
Indian tomato *rasam*, soup (India)
Grilled mangoes seasoned with Tajín (Mexican spice blend with chilli and lime)

Green mango slices dipped in shrimp paste (Vietnam, Philippines)
Salad with mango vinaigrette dressing
Baked brie with mango chutney
Mango habanero chicken wings (Caribbean)
Corn chips with mango salsa (Mexico)

Mains

Amchur chicken (India)
Indian curry with mango chutney (India)
Sinigang (with green mango pulp) (Philippines)
Haitian mango chicken (Haiti)
Chicken tenders with mango-mustard dipping sauce

Side Dishes

Vietnamese green mango salad (Vietnam)
Tropical fruit salad, African after-chop (see Recipes)
Salad Belize (salad mix with mango leaves) (Belize)
Pickled mangoes

Desserts

Mango ice cream (*kulfi*) (India)
Mango sherbet
Mango *barfi* (mango fudge) (India)
Mango pudding
Mango float/Graham Cake (Philippines)
Mango sticky rice (Thailand)

Recipes

Mango Curry

In Farmana in the Ghaggar valley near modern-day Delhi, at an archaeological site, researchers analysed the pots, tools and dental enamel of humans, and were able to identify the starches, vegetables, fruits and spices used 2,000 years ago by the Harappan civilization. Mango fibres were found. Based on this information, food writer Soity Banerjee of the BBC posits what a 2,000-year-old curry may have been.[1]

> 6–7 small aubergines, washed and slit
> 1–3 cm (1 in.) piece of ginger, ground
> 1 fresh turmeric, ground, or ½ tsp turmeric powder
> 1 tbsp raw mango cut into cubes

Combine all ingredients and cook until aubergines are soft. Optional additions, to taste, can include salt, sugar, cumin or basil. *Serves 4*

Mango Pickles
From *The Cook's Oracle: Containing Receipts for Plain Cookery* (London, 1822)

The following will be found something like the real Mango Pickle, especially if the Garlick be used plentifully. To each gallon of the strongest Vinegar put four ounces [100 g] of Curry Powder, same of Flour of Mustard (some rub these together, with half a pint [280 ml] of Salad Oil,) three of Ginger bruised – and two of Turmeric, half a pound [230 g] (when skinned) of Shallots (slightly baked in a Dutch oven), two ounces [60 g] of Garlick, prepared in like manner, a quarter of a pound [110 g] of Salt and two drachms [4 g] of Cayenne Pepper. Put these ingredients into a stone jar, cover

it with a bladder wetted with the pickle, and set it on a trivet by the side of the fire during three days, shaking it up three times a day – it will be ready to receive.
Serves 4

Mango Chutney

Adapted from Marian Fairchild's chutney recipe, *c.* 1930.[2]

10 large ripe mangoes, peeled and diced
10 green mangoes, peeled and diced
80 g (½ cup) seedless raisins
470 ml (½ pint) lime juice
470 ml (½ pint) vinegar
2 chilli peppers
2 garlic cloves, chopped
1 medium onion, chopped
1 tbsp white mustard seeds
1 tbsp celery seeds
1 sweet red bell pepper, diced
1 tsp mustard powder
1 tbsp ground ginger
3 pieces fresh ginger root, grated
1 tbsp whole cloves
50 g (½ cup) lemon peel strips cut into 1-cm (½ in.) lengths
1½ tbsp salt
350 g (1¾ cup) dark brown sugar

Put all ingredients, including the mangoes, into a large bowl and let sit overnight. The next day, place into a large pot and cook, uncovered, on low heat until thick, approximately 3 hours, stirring frequently. Pour into sterilized jars and seal. This will provide 2 quart jars' worth (nearly 2 litres) of chutney.

Mango Sherbet

The word 'sherbet' derives from the Persian word *sharbat*, meaning 'iced fruit drink'. The *Ni'matnama* (The Sultan's Book of Delights) is a late fifteenth-century book of instructions and recipes for food as well as perfumes and medicines prepared for the sultan's court. *Dugh* is a sour milk used to make drinks. An illustrated copy is held in the collection of the British Library.

> Another recipe, for sherbet involves mixing together mango syrup, mango juice, ground cardamoms, cloves and musk. Another recipe, for dugh: put chopped mango into dugh and add palm sugar or salt.[3]

Serves 2

Aam Papad

Aam papad is a traditional Indian fruit leather made from mango pulp. It can be seasoned or sugar can be added. The recipe below uses baby food as the purée and seasons it with Tajín (a Mexican spice blend of chillies, lime and salt).

150 g (½ cup) mango purée (fresh, canned or baby food)
1 tbsp Tajín

Mix the mango purée and Tajín. Pour onto a sheet pan covered with parchment paper or a silicone mat. Cook at 80°C (175°F) for 2 hours. Cut into strips and roll up.
Serves 4

Mango Jalapeño Cornbread Stuffing
Adapted from the National Mango Board (www.mango.org)

5 tbsp unsalted butter
50 g (½ cup) small celery, diced

50 g (½ cup) small white onion, diced
25 g (¼ cup) small jalapeño, diced
2 tbsp garlic, minced
100 g (2 cups) small mango, diced
500 ml (2 cups) chicken stock, divided in half
250 ml (1 cup) buttermilk
4 large eggs
2 tbsp chopped parsley
1 tsp ground coriander
1½ tsp salt
1 tsp ground black pepper
½ tsp poultry seasoning
¼ tsp ground chipotle pepper, optional
400 g (15 oz) sweetcorn, drained
1 kg (6 cups) cooked cornbread, diced

Sauté the onions and celery in butter until soft, about 3 minutes. Add the jalapeños and cook for 1 minute. Add the garlic and diced mangoes and cook for an additional minute. Add half the chicken stock and remove from the heat and allow to cool.

In a large mixing bowl, mix together the remainder of the chicken stock, buttermilk, eggs, parsley and seasonings. Add the cooled vegetables and the corn. Gently mix in the diced cornbread. Pour into a greased 20 × 30 cm (9 × 13 in.) baking pan. Bake at 180°C (350°F) for 45 minutes.
Serves 6

Korean Mango Kimchi and Mango BBQ
Adapted from Da-Hae and Gareth West,
K Food: Korean Home Cooking and Street Food (2016)

Mangoes have only recently been grown in Korea, so many traditional Korean foods have not historically been made with mangoes. The following two recipes adapt Korean BBQ and kimchi to include mangoes. Korean BBQ generally includes a pear paste that has enzymes that break down proteins in the meat. Mangoes also have similar enzymes, and a mango purée, in this case mango baby food, replaces the traditional pear paste. Da-Hae West notes that she spent a summer in JeJe Island, where her family grew mangoes, and she developed this recipe to reflect that enjoyable summer. We have adapted her recipe to accommodate Western tastes that may not prefer or have available fish sauce. A combination of soy sauce, lime juice and rice wine vinegar replaces the fish sauce.

Serves 6

Mango Kimchi

1 mango, peeled, seeded and chopped
¼ onion, finely grated
¼ chilli (preferably long, red Thai chilli)
1 tbsp soy sauce
1 tsp lime juice
1 tsp rice wine vinegar
1 tbsp gochujang, optional
1 tbsp fresh ginger, finely grated
1 glove garlic, minced

Mix everything together and place in a clean glass jar. Let it sit at room temperature to ferment for three days. Refrigerate until needed.

Korean Mango BBQ

2 tbsp onion, chopped
50 ml (¼ cup) soy sauce
50 g (¼ cup) brown sugar
2 tsp sesame oil
½ tsp crushed red pepper
¼ tsp ground ginger
3 gloves garlic
¼ tsp sesame seeds

50 g (⅓ cup) mango purée
450 g (1 lb) pork butt (pork shoulder on the bone), cut into
5-cm (2 in.) cubes
lettuce (for serving)

Place all ingredients (except lettuce) in a pressure-cooker and cook for 45 minutes. Allow to cool. Shred pork and place it back in the cooking liquid. Serve on a lettuce leaf with mango kimchi.

Mango Float

Recipe adapted from 'Mango Float', Food Network Kitchen,
www.foodnetwork.com, accessed 14 March 2022

This celebratory sweet is served in the Philippines, often called Graham Cake for its use of graham crackers.

500 ml (2 cups) whipping cream
1 can condensed milk (14 oz, 400 g)
½ tsp vanilla
250 g (9 oz) graham cracker or digestive biscuit crumbs
3 ripe mangoes, diced

Beat whipping cream, condensed milk and vanilla until doubled in volume. In a 20-cm (8 in.) square pan, layer one-third of the cream mixture, one-third of the graham cracker crumbs and one-third of the diced mangoes; repeat 3 times. Chill overnight.
Serves 6

Haitian Mango Chicken

If possible, for this Haitian dish use the popular mango variety Francis. Recipe adapted from www.food.com.

4 boneless chicken breasts
25 g (¼ cup) green pepper, chopped

2 tbsp butter
50 ml (¼ cup) sherry
100 ml (½ cup) orange juice
200 ml (1 cup) water
1 chicken bouillon cube
250 g (1 cup) mango purée
1 tbsp candied (crystallized) ginger, diced
150 g (1½ cups) mangoes, cubed

Pound the chicken breast to ½ cm (¼ in.) thick. Sauté the chicken in a skillet with the butter and the green peppers. Remove the chicken and deglaze the pan with the sherry. Add the orange juice, water, bouillon cube, mango purée and ginger. Simmer for 10 minutes. Return the chicken to the skillet and add the cubed mango. Heat through. Serve with rice.

Serves 4

West African Mango After-Chop
Adapted from https://oldwayspt.org

A common dessert in West Africa, 'after-chop' is a fresh fruit salad with a bit of coconut, peanuts and honey mixed in. Any favourite in-season fruits can be added, in this case mango.

1 peach, peeled and chopped
1 mango, peeled and chopped
1 tbsp coconut milk
½ tsp honey or maple syrup
1 tbsp chopped peanuts

Place the peeled and diced fruit in a bowl. Drizzle with coconut milk and honey (or maple syrup). Add the peanuts. Stir to coat. Serve immediately or chill.

Serves 2

Mango *Barfi*

Adapted from Nish Kitchen (https://nishkitchen.com)

400 g (1½ cups) mango purée
125 g (1 cup) milk powder
1 can (14 oz, 400 g) condensed milk
1 tbsp ghee
½ tsp ground cardamom
chopped pistachios and/or dried rose petals, for garnish

Over low heat, cook the milk powder and condensed milk for 5 minutes. Add the mango purée, ghee and cardamom, and cook, stirring, for 10 minutes or until the mixture thickens. Pour into a greased pan lined with parchment paper. Garnish with chopped pistachios and dried rose petals. Cool overnight in the refrigerator until set, and then cut into desired shapes.

Serves 8

References

Introduction

1 Fresh Mangoes, www.freshmangoes.us, accessed
  7 September 2023.
2 Ahmed Ali Akbar, 'Inside the Secretive, Semi-Illicit,
  High Stakes World of WhatsApp Mango Importing',
  www.eater.com, 12 August 2021.
3 Ameer Kotecha, 'The Favourite Dishes of Royals',
  The Spectator, www.spectator.co.uk, 5 July 2021.

1 Magnificent Mango: Botany, Production and Health

1 Indu Mehta, 'History of Mango – King of Fruits',
  International Journal of Engineering Science Invention,
  vi/7 (July 2017), pp. 20–24.
2 J. Bates, 'Oilseeds, Spices, Fruits and Flavour in the Indus
  Civilisation', *Journal of Archeological Science*, xxiv (2019),
  pp. 879–87.
3 Noris Ledesma et. al, 'Preliminary Field Adaptation
  and Fruit Characterization of *Mangifera* species
  in Florida', ishs Acta Horticulture: xii International
  Symposium, www.actahort.org, accessed
  24 November 2023.
4 Ian S. E. Bally, '*Mangifera indica* (Mango)', Species Profiles
  for Pacific Island Agroforestry, www.traditionaltree.org,
  April 2006.

5 Sabrina Stierwalt, 'What Do Cashews, Mangoes and
   Poison Ivy Have in Common?', *Scientific American*,
   www.scientificamerican.com, 26 January 2020.
6 'Commodity Briefs: Mango, Mangosteen and Guava',
   Food and Agriculture Organization of the United Nations,
   www.fao.org, accessed 24 November 2023.
7 Mujib Mashal and Hari Kumar, '"Mango Man" Is the Fruit's
   Foremost Poet, Philosopher, Fan and Scientist', *New York
   Times*, www.nytimes.com, 1 July 2022.
8 See Gilda Cordero-Fernando, *The Culinary Culture of the
   Philippines* (Manila, 1976) and Doreen Gamboa Fernandez,
   Tikim: Essays on Philippine Food and Culture (Mandaluyong
   City, 1994).
9 David Shulman, 'The Scent of Memory in Hindu South
   India', *Anthropology and Aesthetics*, 13 (Spring 1987), p. 124.
10 Compound Interest, 'The Chemistry of Mangoes', *SciTech
   Connect*, https://scitechconnect.elsevier.com, 7 August 2017.
11 T.M.M. Malundo et al., 'Sugars and Acids Influence Flavor
   Properties of Mango (*Mango indica*)', *Journal of the American
   Society of Horticultural Science*, CXXVI/1 (2001), pp. 115–20.
12 Urvi Kumbhat, 'On the Complexity of Using the Mango as a
   Symbol in Diasporic Literature', *LitHub*, https://lithub.com,
   8 February 2021.
13 Alberto J. Nunez-Selles et al., 'The Paradox of Natural
   Products as Pharmaceuticals: Experimental Evidence of a
   Mango Stem Bark Extract', *Pharmacological Research*, LV/55
   (2007), pp. 351–8.
14 T. Arumugam et al., 'Fruits and Vegetables as Superfood:
   Scope and Demand', *Pharma Innovation Journal*, X/3 (2021),
   p. 124.
15 Mohammad Saleem et al., 'Antidiabetic Potential of
   Mangifera indica L. cv Anwar Ratol Leaves: Medicinal
   Application of Food Wastes', *Medicina*, LV/7 (2019), p. 353.
16 Megan Ware, 'What to Know about Mangoes', *Medical News
   Today*, www.medicalnewstoday.com, 6 February 2022.

2 Mango Movement

1 Luke Keogh, 'The Wardian Case: How a Simple Box Moved the Plant Kingdom', *Arnoldia*, https://arboretum.harvard.edu, 17 May 2017.

2 'Goa Owes Its Best Mangoes to the Jesuits', *Incredible Goa*, www.incrediblegoa.org, 28 May 2019; Newton Sequeira, 'The Aam Aadmi sj', *Times of India*, https://timesofindia. indiatimes.com, 26 April 2015.

3 James Green, 'The Path They Trod: An Avenue of Mango Trees on the Loango Coast', The Metropolitan Museum of Art, www.metmuseum.org, 11 December 2015.

4 Ibid.

5 Deanne Gayman, 'Wisnicki Lights Up the Legend of Livingstone', *Nebraska Today*, https://news.unl.edu, 23 March 2014.

6 Betty Kibaara and Olivia Karanja, 'What Mangoes in Kenya Can Teach Us About Food Loss', www.rockefellerfoundation.org, 1 May 2018.

7 Jill Collett and Patrick Bowe, *Gardens of the Caribbean* (London, 1998), p. 16.

8 Danielle N. Boaz, 'Obeah, Vagrancy, and the Boundaries of Religious Freedom: Analyzing the Proscription of "Pretending to Possess Supernatural Powers" in the Anglophone Caribbean', *Journal of Law and Religion*, XXXII/3 (November 2017), pp. 423–48.

9 Lindsay Haines, 'Obeah Is a Fact of Life, and Afterlife, in the Caribbean', *New York Times*, www.nytimes.com, 10 September 1972.

10 Patrick McSherry, 'Feeding the Cuban Insurgents', www.spanamwar.com, accessed 13 November 2022.

11 Talek Nantes, 'The 20 Funniest Cuban Expressions and How to Use Them', https://matadornetwork.com, 8 July 2018.

12 Witold Szabłowski, *How to Feed a Dictator* (Warsaw, 2019), p. 175.

13 Anse Chastanet, 'Mango Rules the Caribbean!', https://ansechastanet.com, 29 May 2017.

14 J. Hunelle, '65+ Jamaican Mango Names You Probably Never Knew', https://simplylocal.life, 6 June 2019.

15 Collett and Bowe, *Gardens*, p. 30.

16 Vikram Doctor, 'The Travels of the Mango', *Economic Times*, http://economictimes.indiatimes.com, 3 May 2015.

17 'Nevis All Set to Welcome Mango Festival with Full Enthusiasm in July', *Associates Times*, https://associatestimes.com, 30 June 2022.

18 'Enclosure:Invoice to Robert Cary & Company, 20 September 1759', Founders Online, www.founders.archives.gov, accessed 7 September 2023.

19 Stephen McLeod, *Dining with the Washingtons* (Chapel Hill, NC, 2011), pp. 79–80.

20 'Pickle History Timeline', New York Food Museum, www.nyfoodmuseum.org, accessed 7 September 2023.

21 Akshay Chavan, 'Everyday India, through Ibn Battuta's Eyes', Live History India, www.peepultree.world, 10 April 2023.

22 'History of Early American Landscape Design: The Woodlands', *National Gallery of Art*, https://heald.nga.gov, accessed 22 November 2022.

23 Amanda Harris, *Fruits of Eden: David Fairchild and America's Plant Hunters* (Gainesville, FL, 2015), p. 67.

24 Ibid., pp. 66–7.

25 'Gary Zill's Mango Variety Development Project', Truly Tropical, www.youtube.com, accessed 13 November 2022.

26 Bhaskar Savani, 'The Indian Mango Comes to America', www.chapman.edu, accessed 13 November 2022, and author's discussion with Bhaskar Savani.

3 Mughals and Mangoes

1 See https://adf-foods.com, accessed 15 November 2022.

2 See Ashoka, www.ashoka.org, accessed 15 November 2022.

3 Kusum Budhwar, *Romance of the Mango: The Complete Book of the King of Fruits* (New Delhi, 2002), p. 11.

4 Gaurav Chugani, 'Harsha', World History,
   www.worldhistory.org, 14 March 2016.
5 Maghulika Dash, 'A Complete History of the Mango:
   From the Times of Mauryas to Mughals', Swarajya,
   https://swarajyamag.com, 9 June 2016.
6 Ashutosh Potnis, 'Of Mangoes and the Mughals',
   https://ashutoshpotnis.wixsite.com, 21 May 2020.
7 Ibid.
8 Budhwar, *Romance*, p. 14.
9 William Dalrymple, *The Last Mughal: The Fall
   of a Dynasty: Delhi, 1857* [2006] (New York, 2008), p. 103.
10 Quoted in Potnis, 'Of Mangoes'.
11 Ibid.
12 Ibid.
13 Budhwar, *Romance*, p. 15.
14 Ibid., p. 16.
15 Diya Kohli, 'Two of India's Most Expensive Mangoes that
   You've Probably Not Heard Of', *Condé Nast Traveller*,
   www.cntraveller.in, 7 June 2021.
16 Mujib Mashal and Hari Kumar, '"Mango Man" Is the
   Fruit's Foremost Poet, Philosopher, Fan and Scientist',
   New York Times, www.nytimes.com, 1 July 2022.
17 Serish Nanisetti, 'Mango, the King of Summers',
   The Hindu, www.thehindu.com, 12 May 2018.
18 Budhwar, *Romance*, p. 16.
19 Salma Yusuf Husain, 'No One Could See Shah Jahan Eat.
   But a Portuguese Priest once Snuck in and Here's What
   He Saw', *The Print*, https://theprint.in, 2 June 2019.
20 Dash, 'A Complete History'.
21 Husain, 'No One Could See Shah Jahan Eat'.
22 Niccolao Manucci, 'Storia do Mogor; or, Mogul India
   1653–1708, Chapter XVIII', available at Internet Archive,
   https://archive.org, accessed 15 November 2022.
23 Dalrymple, *The Last Mughal*, p. 3.
24 Sandra Wagner-Wright, 'Taj Mahal Gardens and
   Lord Curzon', www.sandrawagnerwright.com,
   12 October 2015.

25 Vandana Menon, 'Even a Pandemic Can't Stop the Indian Mango', *The Juggernaut*, www.thejuggernaut.com, 15 May 2020.

26 Naveed Siddiqui, 'FO Denies "Misleading" Reports of Pakistani Mangoes Gifted to Foreign Dignitaries', *Dawn*, www.dawn.com, 13 June 2021.

4 The British and European Connection to Mango

1 Avinash Lohana, 'Ali Fazel Sends Fresh Alphonso Mangoes to His Victoria & Abdul Co-Star Judi Dench', *Mumbai Mirror*, https://mumbaimirror.indiatimes.com, 22 May 2018.

2 Prashant Powle, 'Why Mango Is Called Bathroom Fruit', https://alphonsomango.in, 19 February 2022.

3 See Babushahi Bureau, 'Amb-Choop Mango Mela: Novel and Unique Way to Remember Dr MS Randhawa', www.babushahi.com, 7 July 2019.

4 M. S. Randhawa, *Flowering Trees in India* (New Delhi, 1957), p. 44.

5 Marianne North, 'Foliage, Flowers and Young Fruit of the Mango', Royal Botanic Gardens, Kew, https://images.kew.org, accessed 3 November 2022.

6 Anne Brassey, *A Voyage in the 'Sunbeam': Our Home on the Ocean for Eleven Months* [1878] (New York, 2014), p. 38.

7 Ibid., p. 238.

8 Maria Graham Callcott, *Journal of a Residence in India* [1812], ebook, https://fiftywordsforsnow.com, accessed 22 November 2022.

9 Isabella L. Bird, *The Hawaiian Archipelago* [1875], ebook, www.gutenberg.org, accessed 7 September 2023.

10 Hugo McCafferty, 'Sicily Adapts to Climate Change with Tropical Fruits', Fine Dining Lovers, www.finedininglovers.com, 16 April 2009.

11 Galway Spirits, www.galwayspirits.com, accessed 22 November 2022.

12 Kiersten Hickman, 'The One Food the Royal Family Can't Eat While Traveling', Taste of Home, www.tasteofhome.com, 20 March 2019.

13 Diane Stoneback, 'Fixing Meals Fit for a Princess', *Baltimore Sun*, www.baltimoresun.com, 22 August 2007.

14 Ruth Styles, 'Tins of Tuna, Woolly Hats and a Model of a Surface to Air Missile: The Lavish (and Often Bizarre) Gifts Given to the Queen and other Royals in 2014 Revealed', *Daily Mail*, www.dailymail.co.uk, 14 January 2015.

15 Sybil Kapoor, 'Handle with Care: Why Mangoes are Like a Woman's Breast', *The Guardian*, www.theguardian.com, 3 June 2000.

5 Mao, Mangoes and the East

1 'China's Curious Cult of the Mango', BBC News, www.bbc.co.uk, 11 February 2016.

2 Ibid.

3 Ibid.

4 Alfreda Murck, ed., *Mao's Golden Mangoes and the Cultural Revolution*, exh. cat., Museum Rietberg (Zurich, 2013), p. 74.

5 'Mango Market Continues to Rise in China', Fresh Plaza, www.freshplaza.com, 1 June 2022.

6 Dan Siekman, 'Guangxi Mangos Hit Peak Production; Prices Are Strong', Produce Report, www.producereport.com, 29 July 2019.

7 Q. B. Chen, 'Perspectives on the Mango Industry in Mainland China', ISHS Acta Horticulturae 992: IX International Mango Symposium, www.actahort.org, accessed 12 November 2022.

8 'Visit First Mango Festival in China', CGTN Live, www.youtube.com, accessed 12 November 2022.

9 Gao Yun, 'China Breeds the World's First "Space Mangoes"', CGTN, http://news.cgtn.com, 21 March 2017.

10 Julia Janicki et al., 'Taiwan's Mangoes', Taiwan Data Stories, www.taiwandatastories.com, accessed 12 November 2022.

11 'How Much Do You Know about the Mangos in Taiwan?',
    Taiwan Food Tour, www.justaiwantour.com, accessed
    12 November 2022.

12 Ibid.

13 Ibid.

14 Lee Ji-yoon, 'Warming Jeju Seeks New Opportunities', *Korea
    Herald*, www.koreaherald.com, 18 July 2010.

15 'Gyeongnam Apple Mango Harvest in Full Swing', *Haps
    Magazine Korea*, www.hapskorea.com, 10 May 2022.

16 Srishti Dutta, 'World's Most Expensive Mango', *India Times*,
    www.indiatimes.com, 25 August 2023.

17 'Two Premium Mangoes Sell for Record Amount in
    Southwest Japan Auction', Fresh Plaza, www.freshplaza.com,
    15 April 2022.

6 Sugary Sweet to Sharply Sour: Philippines, Southeast Asia, Australia and South Pacific

1 Doreen Gamboa Fernandez, 'Mangoes and Maytime', in
   Tikim: Essays on Philippine Food and Culture (Mandaluyong
   City, 1994), p. 52.

2 'Mangoes in the Philippines', Crop Life, https://croplife.org,
   accessed 12 November 2022.

3 'Philippine Mango Industry Roadmap 2017–2022', Philippine
   Department of Agriculture, www.da.gov.ph, accessed
   12 November 2022, p. 2.

4 Amy Besa and Romy Dorotan, *Memories of Philippine
   Kitchens* (New York, 2006), p. 29.

5 'Philippine Mango Industry Roadmap', p. 1.

6 Karen Gwee, 'MILLI Officially Releases Coachella-Viral Song
   "Mango Sticky Rice"', *NME*, www.nme.com, 20 May 2022.

7 'Mango Art Festival, 2022 Bangkok', www.mangoartfestival.
   com, accessed 12 November 2022.

8 Jen Hoang, 'Sauce for Sour Mangoes', Jenuine Cuisine,
   www.jenuinecuisine.com, accessed 8 September 2023.

9 'Growing Cambodian Mango', www.gocambodia.com, accessed 7 September 2023.
10 'Cambodia Launches First Direct Shipment of Fresh Mangoes to China', www.china.org.cn, 7 May 2021.
11 'Malacca Delite, the Sweet Mango of Southern State', *Sun Daily*, www.thesundaily.my, 6 July 2019.
12 Jane Ryan, 'A Short History of Growing Mangoes in Australia', Difford's Guide, www.diffordsguide.com, accessed 12 November 2022.
13 '"Wild Mango", One of the Earliest-Known Plant Foods Eaten in Australia, Next Big Thing', *Australian Geographic*, www.australiangeographic.com.au, 2 June 2022.
14 Ryan, 'A Short History'.
15 Ibid.
16 Ibid.
17 Daniel Fitzgerald, 'Picking Mangoes at Night Works for Northern Territory Mango Farm, Despite Bats and Bugs', ABC News, www.abc.net.au, 14 December 2015.
18 Richard A. Hamilton et al., *Mango Cultivars in Hawaii*, College of Tropical Agriculture and Human Resources (Honolulu, HI, 1992), p. 1.
19 Brooke Wong, 'The History of Crack Seed in Hawaii', Snack Hawaii, www.snackhawaii.com, 30 June 2016.
20 'Mr Mango Crack', Pevgrow, https://pevgrow.com, accessed 12 November 2022.

7 Mangoes, Metaphors and Meanings

1 Cynthia Thuma, *The Mongo Mango Cookbook and Everything You Ever Wanted to Know About Mangoes* (Sarasota, FL, 2001).
2 Kusum Budhwar, *Romance of the Mango: The Complete Book of the King of Fruits* (New Delhi, 2002), p. 63.
3 Lyndsey Steven, 'Mango Girls: Trees Saving Lives of Girls in India', *Emirates Woman*, https://emirateswoman.com, 26 September 2014.
4 Ibid.

5 Thuma, *Mongo Mango Cookbook*, p. 18.
6 'Tying Mango Leaves', www.indianmirror.com, accessed
   13 November 2022.
7 Lipi Upadhyay, '#Diwali2017: Why Does Everyone Decorate
   Their Homes with Marigold Flowers and Mango Leaves?',
   India Today, www.indiatoday.in, 18 October 2017.
8 See 'Ugadi 2021: Know All About Ugadi Pachadi, the Special
   Delicacy of the Day', www.news18.com, 13 April 2021.
9 'The Art of South and Southeast Asia', The Metropolitan
   Museum of Art, www.metmuseum.org, accessed
   13 November 2022.
10 Allan Hunt Badiner, 'Vaisali: First Stop to Enlightenment',
   Tricycle: The Buddhist Review (Fall 2004), available at
   https://tricycle.org, accessed 23 November 2023.
11 Ven. Mingun Sayadaw, 'The Great Chronicle of Buddhas:
   Part 3 Buddha's Performance of Miracles (Pāṭihāriya)',
   available at www.wisdomlib.org, accessed 13 November 2022.
12 'Mahakapi Jutaka: The Great Monkey King', *Encyclopedia
   of Buddhism*, https://encyclopediaofbuddhism.org, accessed
   7 September 2023.
13 'AbbhantaraJataka (#281)', available at www.thejatakatales.
   com, accessed 6 November 2023.
14 'Ambika', V&A Museum, https://collections.vam.ac.uk,
   accessed 27 November 2022.
15 See 'Kamadeva and His Mount Parrot', at
   www.exoticindiaart.com, accessed 13 November 2022.
16 'The Ashoka', https://venetiaansell.wordpress.com,
   17 April 2010.
17 Yogendra Yadav, 'Mango in Perspective of Mahatma Gandhi',
   https://gandhiking.ning.com, 15 July 2012.
18 Ibid.
19 Stephanie Vermillion, 'Inside Mahatma Gandhi's Search
   for the Perfect Diet', www.mkgandhi.org, accessed
   13 November 2022.
20 'The Ashoka'.
21 Radhika Oberoi, 'Exploring Mangoes as Metaphor in South
   Asian Writing', *The Wire*, www.thewire.in, 4 July 2017.

22 Amulya Malladi, *The Mango Season* (New York, 2003),
p. 170.

23 Marivi Soliven, *The Mango Bride* (New York, 2013), p. 259.

24 Mary Kate McGrath, 'Ariana Grande's Mango Tweet Is the
Fruit before Boyfriends Message You Didn't Know You
Needed', *Bustle*, www.bustle.com, 17 March 2019.

25 'Tagore: When I Called You in Your Garden Mango Blooms
Were Rich in Fragrance', Byron's Muse, https://byronsmuse.
wordpress.com, 21 February 2022.

26 Tarfia Faizullah, 'Self-Portrait as Mango', https://poems.com,
7 June 2021.

27 'Kakubha Ragini', Smithsonian National Museum of Asian
Art, www.ragamalaexhibit.com, accessed 7 September 2023.

28 Diana Coupland, 'Under the Mango Tree' (from *Dr. No*),
Song Lyrics, www.songlyrics.com, accessed 13 November 2022.

29 Sheila O'Malley, 'Gauguin: Voyage to Tahiti', Roger Ebert,
www.rogerebert.com, 11 July 2018.

30 David Edelstein, 'The Biopic *Gauguin* Is Surprisingly Dull,
Considering Its Subject', *Vulture*, www.vulture.com, 11 July 2018.

31 'The Hunt for the Origins of Indian Yellow Pigment',
www.underthemoonlight.ca, 20 April 2021.

32 Jasvinder Kaur, 'How the Bita or Ambi became Scottish
Paisley', www.lifestyle.livemint.com, 21 February 2022.

33 See 'Mango', www.emojipedia.org, accessed 7 September 2023.

8 Mango Miracle:
Future of Mangoes

1 'How Mangos Move Menu Items', *Restaurant Business*,
www.restaurantbusinessonline.com, 28 March 2019.

2 Ibid.

3 See 'Ataulfo Mangoes', www.specialtyproduce.com,
accessed 7 September 2023.

4 See 'Mango By Products – Converting Mango Wastes
into Valuable Products', www.abcfruits.net, accessed
24 May 2022.

5   See 'Mango Farming in Southern California',
    www.theproducenerd.com, 27 August 2021.
6   'TechnoServe's Haiti Hope Project: Message in
    a Mango', www.3blmedia.com, 7 June 2016.
7   UN Women, 'Mango Farmers in Kenya Get Access
    to New Technology to Counter Post-Harvest Losses',
    United Nations, www.un.org, accessed 11 November 2022.
8   'About Us', Angkor Harvest, https://angkorharvest.com,
    accessed 11 November 2022.
9   Shyam Singh et al., 'Ultra-High Density Plantation
    of Mango-New Technology for Increasing the Income
    of the Farmers', *Indian Farmer*, IV/5 (May 2017), pp. 368–75.
    'Ultra High Density Plantation (UHDP) Mango', *AgroGuide*,
    www.agroguide.nl.
10 Zainuri, Taslim Sjah, Nurrachman and Candra Ayu, 'Mango
    Off-Season Technology (MOST): Innovative, Applicable,
    Adaptive to Climate Change, and Brings Many Positive
    Impacts', *AIP Conference Proceedings*, MMCXCIX/1
    (23 December 2019), available at https://pubs.aip.org.

Recipes

1   Soity Banerjee, 'Cooking the World's Oldest Known Curry',
    BBC News, www.bbc.co.uk/news, 22 June 2016.
2   'Mango Season Makes Way for Magnificent Chutney',
    Fairfield Tropical Botanic Garden Virtual Herbarium,
    www.virtualherbarium.org, accessed 7 September 2023.
3   Norah Tiley, trans., *The Ni'matnama Manuscript of the
    Sultans of Mandu*, *The Sultan's Book of Delights* (London,
    2005), p. 28.

Select Bibliography

Alford, Jeffrey, and Naomi Duguid, *Mangoes and Curry Leaves:
    Culinary Travels through the Great Continent* (Toronto, 2005)
Budhwar, Kusum, *Romance of the Mango: The Complete Book
    of the King of Fruits* (New Delhi, 2002)
Fry, Carolyn, Sue Seddon and Gail Vines, *The Last Great Plant
    Hunt: The Story of Kew's Millennium Seed Bank* (London,
    2011)
Gollner, Adam Leith, *The Fruit Hunters: A Story of Nature,
    Adventure, Commerce and Obsession* (New York, 2008)
Harris, Amanda, *Fruits of Eden: David Fairchild and America's
    Plant Hunters* (Gainesville, FL, 2015)
Jaffrey, Madhur, *Climbing the Mango Trees: A Memoir of a
    Childhood in India* (New York, 2005)
Karetnick, Jen, *Mango* (Gainesville, FL, 2014)
Khanna, Vikas, and Hari Nayak, *Mango Mia: Celebrating
    the Tropical World of Mangoes* (West Conshohocken,
    PA, 2005)
Palter, Robert, *The Duchess of Malfi's Apricots and other Literary
    Fruits* (Columbia, SC, 2002)
Singh, Lal Behari, *The Mango: Botany, Cultivation, and
    Utilization* (New York, 1960)
Stone, Daniel, *The Food Explorer: The Adventures of the
    Globe-Trotting Botanist Who Transformed What America
    Eats* (New York, 2018)
Susser, Allen, *The Great Mango Book: A Guide with Recipes*
    (Berkeley, CA, 2001)

Thuma, Cynthia, *The Mongo Mango Cookbook and Everything You Ever Wanted to Know About Mangoes* (Sarasota, FL, 2001)

Children's Books Featuring Mangoes

Amin, Hidayah, *The Mango Tree* (Singapore, 2013)
Hanson, Regina, *A Season for Mangoes* (New York, 2005)
Kim, Tae-yeon, *Mango Trees* (Minneapolis, MN, 2015)
Paikai, Tommy, *Too Many Mangoes: A Story About Sharing* (Honolulu, HI, 2009)
Rumford, James, *Mango Rain* (Cedar Key, FL, 2011)
Sacre, Antonio, *A Mango in the Hand: A Story Told through Proverbs* (New York, 1968)
Sharma, Natasha, *The Good Indian Child's Guide to Eating Mangoes* (Noida, 2018)
Shetty, Malavika, *The Sweetest Mango* (Chennai, 2012)

Sari-Mango Literature

Malladi, Amulya, *Mango Season* (New York, 2004)
Manicka, Rani, *The Rice Mother* (New York, 2003)
Soliven, Marivi, *The Mango Bride* (London, 2013)

Websites and Associations

Agricultural and Processed Food Products Export Development
Authority (APEDA)
(Ministry of Commerce and Industry, Government of India)
www.apeda.gov.in

Australian Mangoes
www.industry.mangoes.net.au

Business Fights Poverty (collaboration between the Coca-Cola
Company and India's mango farmers)
https://businessfightspoverty.org

Fresh mango source, with many international varieties
www.freshmangoes.us

Fresh Plaza (global trade media platform for the fresh produce
industry)
www.freshplaza.com

International Society for Horticultural Science
www.ishs.org

National Mango Board
www.mango.org

Philippine Mango Industry Roadmap, 2017–22
www.da.gov.ph

Tree Journey
https://treejourney.com

zzMangoes (importer)
www.zzmango.com

Mango Festivals

Australia
Bondi Beach Mango Festival, November
Mango Madness Festival – Darwin City, November

Caribbean
Mango Madness St Lucia, June
Nevis Mango Festival, July
St Croix Mango Melee and Tropical Fruit Festival, July

China
Baise City, Guangxi Zhuang Autonomous Region, July

India
Global Kokan Mango Festival, also called the Mango Fleea,
Mumbai, April
Delhi International Mango Festival, July
Mango Mela – Pinjore, July

Pakistan
Mango Festival – introducing imported Pakistani mangoes to new
markets, Dubai, Shanghai other cities, various months

Philippines
Dinamulag Festival/Zambales Mango Festival, March or April
Guimaras Mango Festival/Manggahan Festival, May

Thailand
Chachoengsao Mango Festival, near Bangkok, April
Chiang Mai Mango Fair, May

Mango Fest Key West, Florida, June
Fairchild Botanic Gardens Mango Festival, Miami, Florida, July
Mango Mania, Pine Island's Tropical Fruit Fair, Florida, July
Mango Festival Sheraton Kona Resort, Kona Island, Hawaii, August

Acknowledgements

We are indebted to mangovores worldwide who have shared their intense love and knowledge of this much adored fruit. Our thanks go out to researchers Noris Ledesma and Richard Campbell of Homestead, Florida, and Bhaskar Savani of Fort Washington, Pennsylvania. We so enjoyed the enthusiasm of DJ Ruscik, Mango Queen of Pine Island, Florida.

We learned so much from mango growers Robert Moehling in Homestead, Florida, Stephanie Guillou and Giuseppe Forenze in Sicily, Veny Marti of Martex Farms in Puerto Rico, Louise King of the Fruit and Space Park in Homestead, Florida, Sally and Denis Pead in Málaga, Spain, and Marsela McGrane of the National Mango Board. We learned about wholesale mango sales from Michael Lombardo of Pinto Brothers Wholesale Produce Market, Philadelphia, Pennsylvania.

We greatly appreciate friends in social and print media who champion culinary history, including Nicky Twilley of *Gastropod*, Janet Irvin of *Write Side*, Gretchen Schmidt of *Edible South Florida* and Dean Jones of *Well-Seasoned Librarian*.

We enjoyed the mango creations in the restaurants of many chefs who feature this amazing fruit, including The Mango Tree in Cincinnati, Ohio, Mango Mangeaux in Hampton, Virginia, Hosu restaurant in Taipei, Taiwan, Catalina Oliver Ors restaurant in Palma de Mallorca, Spain, and Mango Mango Desserts in Philadelphia, Pennsylvania.

Our thanks to all our many Philadelphia and Cincinnati friends who dutifully scouted for mango references and photos, including

Joanne Bening and Sandy Kheradi. Paula Roberts provided helpful editorial assistance. Kathryn Lorenz of Lorenz Language Consultants was an early reader of the book and gave us editing and proofreading assistance, as did the Friends and Books book club of Cincinnati. Singapore friends Shadow Paul, Charlotte Chu and Eve Felder made this mango journey such a pleasure. Our friend Marie Coreces shared her favourite mangoes.

Amy Salter and Alex Ciobanu at Reaktion Books ably guided us through the publishing process.

Lastly and most importantly, thank you to our patient families, including budding mangovore granddaughters Josie and Eliza Kirker, who make wonderful mango lassis. Husbands Tom Kirker and John Kachuba accompanied us on all our culinary journeys with good cheer.

Photo Acknowledgements

The author and publishers wish to express their thanks to the sources listed below for illustrative material and/or permission to reproduce it. Some locations of artworks are also given below, in the interest of brevity:

Alamy Stock Photo: pp. 26 (Jeffrey Isaac Greenberg 5+), 43 (Ramon Espinosa/Associated Press), 131 (Dinodia Photos RM); courtesy the artist: p. 45; Baltimore Museum of Art, MD: p. 13; from Michał Boym, *Flora sinensis* (Vienna, 1656), photo Harvard University Botany Libraries, Cambridge, MA: p. 18; British Library, London (MS Or 3714, fol. 396r): p. 62; Chester Beatty, Dublin: p. 37; The Cleveland Museum of Art, OH: pp. 69, 128; Flickr: p. 97 (photo sanmai, CC BY 2.0); Freer Gallery of Art, National Museum of Asian Art, Smithsonian Institution, Washington, DC: p. 65; Getty Images: pp. 9 (Karwai Tang), 30 (Maryke Vermaak/AFP), 70 (Burhaan Kinu/Hindustan Times), 84 (Anwar Hussein), 107 (Kevin Mazur); courtesy HoSu restaurant, Taipei: p. 94; iStock.com: pp. 6 (ValentynVolkov), 85 (thesomegirl); The J. Paul Getty Museum, Los Angeles: p. 126; photos Constance L. Kirker: pp. 8, 10, 21, 22, 25, 28, 29, 48, 54, 63, 66, 74, 77, 82, 83, 90, 92, 93, 98, 104, 109, 110, 114, 119, 120, 140, 141, 142, 144, 145; The Metropolitan Museum of Art, New York: p. 136; courtesy National Mango Board, Orlando, FL: p. 53; photo Mary Newman: p. 116; Royal Botanic Gardens, Kew, London: p. 78; Royal Collection Trust/© His Majesty King Charles III 2024: pp. 72, 79; USDA Pomological Watercolor Collection, Rare and Special Collections, National Agricultural Library, Beltsville, MD: pp. 15, 55; photo

Maria Villafane: p. 143; from N. B. Ward, *On the Growth of Plants in Closely Glazed Cases* (London, 1852), photo Gray Herbarium Library, Harvard University, Cambridge, MA: p. 36; Wikimedia Commons: pp. 39 (photo Halidtz, CC BY-SA 4.0), 60 (photo Bpilgrim, CC BY-SA 2.5), 88 (photo Daderot, public domain), 102–3 (photo Ranieljosecastaneda, CC BY-SA 4.0), 124 (photo Hiart, public domain), 125 (photo Biswarup Ganguly, CC BY 3.0).

Index

italic numbers refer to illustrations; **bold** to recipes